250 best
Cobblers,
Custards, Cupcakes,
Breads and more

For complete cataloguing information, see page 189.

Disclaimer

Design & Production: PageWave Graphics Inc.
Editor: Sue Sumeraj
Proofreader: Sheila Wawanash
Index: Gillian Watts
Photography: Mark T. Shapiro
Food Styling: Kate Bush
Prop Styling: Charlene Erricson

Cover image: Strawberry-Rhubarb Cobbler (see recipe, page 34)

The publisher and author wish to express their appreciation to the following supplier of props used in the food photography:

Gourmet Settings Inc.
245 West Beaver Creek Road, Unit 10
Richmond Hill, Ontario L4B 1L1
Tel: 1-800-551-2649
www.gourmetsettings.com

We acknowledge the financial support of the Government of Canada through the Book Publishing Industry Development Program (BPIDP) for our publishing activities.

Published by Robert Rose Inc.
120 Eglinton Avenue East, Suite 800, Toronto, Ontario, Canada M4P 1E2
Tel: (416) 322-6552 Fax: (416) 322-6936

Printed in Canada

1 2 3 4 5 6 7 8 9 CPL 12 11 10 09 08 07 06 05 04

Contents

Introduction

There is nothing like homemade cupcakes, cobblers, custards, puddings, etc. It may seem to take so much longer than buying quick, ready-made, but it is well worth the extra wait, and these are really not difficult to make. The only difficult part is really waiting for your baking to cool, set, bake or chill in the refrigerator before you dig in and enjoy your masterpiece, which can range from plain to fancy, and basic ingredients to gloriously rich and gooey.

Years ago, I remember asking a lady that I admired as a terrific cook and baker, just what was the difference between all of these desserts, namely ones such as cobblers, crisps, crumbles, brown betties, crunches, etc. I was very familiar with puddings and custards and, of course, cupcakes, but the others I found confusing. She explained to me that most of these desserts consisted of fruit topped with a biscuit type of dough, which I had made many times and knew consisted mainly of flour, sugar and butter or margarine.

She went on to explain that when making a cobbler recipe the fruit filling is hidden under a biscuit topping, which is dropped by spoonfuls on top of the fruit and has a sugared top. It makes a lumpy surface, similar to a street paved with round stones, and was therefore called a "cobbler," like the old cobblestone streets. A crisp has a fruit filling topped with a crunchy mixture of butter, flour, sugar, spices, nuts and sometimes oatmeal. Brown betties, and it can be other fruit besides apples, have the fruit layered with buttery bread crumbs. Crumbles are similar to crisps and have the same type of topping, without oatmeal.

Rice puddings, made with rice, eggs, cream and sometimes raisins, and bread puddings, consisting of cubes, chunks or slices of day-old breads (French or egg bread are also delicious), have been around for a long time and are still favorites, as are steamed puddings, which have traditionally been a part of Christmas dinners for many years. Custards are mainly beaten eggs mixed with milk or cream, sugar and some type of flavoring and are either cooked on the stove top or baked in the oven. Crème brûlée is usually a custard, or can be a pudding, topped with a generous amount of sugar and broiled to make a crisp, browned top crust.

All of these recipes can be made into many different assorted desserts. One of my favorites has always been trifle, and most are quick and simple to make. Some of the funny or odd names go back to early American cooking, with an English influence, and have resulted in names like grunts, slumps, buckles, pandowdies, bubbles, squeaks, and so on. I have always concentrated on the more familiar ones, as you will find in this book.

Whether you are a novice or a long-time baker, and even though you may be more familiar with baking cakes, pies and muffins, once you start experimenting with other baking recipes, such as the ones in this book, and see how easy and delicious they are, I hope you will be inspired to try many more.

Happy Baking!

— *Esther*

Cupcakes

Angel Food Cupcakes

MAKES 24 CUPCAKES

12	egg whites (use large eggs)	12
1½ tsp	cream of tartar	7 mL
¼ tsp	salt	1 mL
1 cup	granulated sugar	250 mL
2 tsp	vanilla	10 mL
1 cup	cake flour	250 mL
½ cup	confectioner's (icing) sugar, sifted	125 mL
	Can of prepared frosting	

- *Preheat oven to 375°F (190°C)*
- *24 muffin cups, lined with paper baking*

1. In a large mixer bowl, on medium speed, beat egg whites, cream of tartar and salt until mixture is foamy. Turn speed up to high and continue beating until soft peaks form. Gradually add sugar by spoonfuls, then vanilla, beating until stiff, glossy peaks form.

2. In a small bowl, combine flour and confectioner's sugar. Sift over the beaten egg whites and fold into mixture until flour is well incorporated and no longer visible.

3. Spoon batter into prepared muffin cups, filling to top, and bake in preheated oven for 20 to 25 minutes, or until a toothpick inserted in the center of a cupcake comes out clean and dry.

4. Remove from pan and cool on wire rack. When completely cooled, frost with your favorite frosting or sprinkle some confectioner's sugar over tops of cupcakes.

Banana Cupcakes

MAKES 12 CUPCAKES

1 cup	granulated sugar	250 mL
½ cup	butter or margarine, softened	125 mL
2	eggs	2
1 tsp	vanilla	5 mL
1¾ cups	all-purpose flour	425 mL
½ tsp	salt	2 mL
½ tsp	baking powder	2 mL
½ tsp	baking soda	2 mL
3	large ripe bananas, cut into 1-inch (2.5 cm) chunks	3
⅓ cup	sour cream	75 mL

- *Preheat oven to 400°F (200°C)*
- *12 muffin cups, greased or paper-lined*

1. In a large mixer bowl, cream sugar and butter until light and fluffy. Add eggs one at a time, beating after each addition. Beat in vanilla.

2. In a medium bowl, sift together flour, salt, baking powder and baking soda.

3. In a blender or food processor, purée bananas and sour cream until smooth.

4. Add flour mixture and banana mixture alternately to the egg mixture, stirring only until blended and moistened. Spoon into prepared muffin cups.

5. Bake in preheated oven for 15 to 20 minutes, or until a toothpick inserted into the center of a cupcake comes out clean and dry. Cool in pan for 10 minutes, then remove onto wire rack to cool completely.

Candy Apple Cupcakes

MAKES 12 CUPCAKES

1 1/3 cups	all-purpose flour	325 mL
1 1/2 tsp	ground cinnamon	7 mL
1 tsp	baking powder	5 mL
1/2 tsp	baking soda	2 mL
1/2 tsp	salt	2 mL
1/2 tsp	ground nutmeg	2 mL
Pinch	ground cloves	Pinch
3/4 cup	granulated sugar	175 mL
1/3 cup	butter or margarine, softened	75 mL
2	eggs	2
1 tsp	vanilla	5 mL
3/4 cup	sweetened applesauce (or use 2 medium apples, peeled and chopped)	175 mL

Topping

20	caramels	20
3 tbsp	milk	45 mL
1 cup	finely chopped nuts (pecans or walnuts)	250 mL
12	Popsicle sticks	12

- *Preheat oven to 350°F (180°C)*
- *12 muffin cups, greased or paper-lined*

1. In a large bowl, combine flour, cinnamon, baking powder, baking soda, salt, nutmeg and cloves. Mix well.
2. In a large mixer bowl, on medium speed, cream sugar and butter. Add eggs and vanilla and beat until well mixed.
3. Add flour mixture alternately with applesauce into the egg mixture and mix until just blended and moistened. Do not over-mix.
4. Spoon into prepared baking cups and bake in preheated oven for 25 minutes, or until a toothpick inserted in the center of a cupcake comes out clean and dry. Cool in pan for 10 minutes, then remove from pan and cool completely on wire rack.
5. *Prepare topping:* In a small saucepan, over low heat, cook caramels and milk until smooth. Spread over tops of cupcakes. Sprinkle chopped nuts over top. Insert a Popsicle stick into the center of each cupcake.

Everyday Cupcakes

MAKES 24 CUPCAKES

1 2/3 cups	sifted cake flour	400 mL
1 1/2 tsp	baking powder	7 mL
1 cup	granulated sugar	250 mL
1/2 cup	butter or margarine, softened (or shortening)	125 mL
2	eggs, well beaten	2
1/2 cup	milk	125 mL
1 tsp	vanilla (or lemon extract)	5 mL

- *Preheat oven to 350°F (180°C)*
- *24 muffin cups, greased or paper-lined*

1. In a large bowl, sift together cake flour and baking powder.
2. In a medium mixer bowl, on medium speed, cream sugar and butter until light and fluffy. Beat in eggs.
3. Add flour mixture to creamed mixture alternately with the milk, a small amount at a time, beating after each addition. Add vanilla. Pour into prepared muffin cups, filling three-quarters full.
4. Bake in preheated oven for 20 to 25 minutes, or until a toothpick inserted into the center of a cupcake comes out clean and dry. Cool on wire rack. Frost with your favorite frosting.

Brownie Pecan Cupcakes

MAKES 12 CUPCAKES

½ cup	butter or margarine	125 mL
3	squares (each 1 oz/30 g) unsweetened baking chocolate	3
2	eggs	2
1 cup	granulated sugar	250 mL
1 ½ tsp	vanilla	7 mL
⅔ cup	all-purpose flour	150 mL
¼ tsp	baking powder	1 mL
¼ cup	milk	50 mL
½ cup	finely chopped nuts (walnuts or pecans)	125 mL

- *Preheat oven to 350°F (180°C)*
- *12 muffin cups, greased or paper-lined*

1. In a small saucepan, over low heat, melt butter and chocolate, stirring until melted. Remove from heat and set aside to cool.

2. In a medium mixer bowl, on high speed, beat eggs until frothy. Gradually beat in sugar until mixture is pale yellow in color and thick. Lower speed to low and add chocolate mixture and vanilla.

3. In a small bowl, mix together flour and baking powder. Beat flour mixture into egg mixture alternately with the milk. Stir in nuts. Spoon into prepared muffin cups, filling about three-quarters full.

4. Bake in preheated oven for 20 to 25 minutes, or until a toothpick inserted in the center comes out only slightly wet. Cool in pan for about 10 minutes, remove and cool completely on wire rack.

Maraschino Cherry Cupcakes

MAKES 12 CUPCAKES

¾ cup	granulated sugar	175 mL
½ cup	butter or margarine, softened	125 mL
2	eggs	2
1 ⅓ cups	all-purpose flour	325 mL
1 tsp	baking powder	5 mL
¼ cup	syrup from jar of maraschino cherries	50 mL
¼ cup	milk	50 mL
1 tsp	vanilla	5 mL
¼ tsp	almond extract	1 mL
¼ cup	drained and finely chopped maraschino cherries (about 15 to 20 cherries)	50 mL

- *Preheat oven to 350°F (180°C)*
- *12 muffin cups, greased or paper-lined*

1. In a large mixer bowl, cream sugar and butter until light and fluffy. Beat in eggs one at a time, just until blended.

2. In a small bowl, whisk flour and baking powder until blended.

3. In another small bowl, combine cherry syrup, milk, vanilla and almond extract.

4. Beat flour mixture into creamed mixture alternately with the cherry syrup mixture, beating on low just until blended. Stir in cherries and mix well. Spoon into prepared muffin cups, filling about three-quarters full.

5. Bake in preheated oven for 20 to 25 minutes, or until golden brown and a toothpick inserted in the center comes out clean and dry. Cool in pan for 10 minutes, then remove and cool completely on wire rack.

Rich Chocolate Cupcakes

MAKES 12 CUPCAKES

½ cup	butter or shortening	125 mL
1 cup	granulated sugar	250 mL
2	egg yolks	2
2 cups	all-purpose flour	500 mL
2 tsp	baking powder	10 mL
¼ tsp	baking soda	1 mL
¼ tsp	salt	1 mL
¾ cup	milk	175 mL
1 tsp	vanilla	5 mL
3	squares (each 1 oz/30 g) unsweetened baking chocolate, melted	3
2	egg whites	2

White Fluffy Frosting

1 lb	confectioner's (icing) sugar, sifted (about 3½ to 4 cups/875 mL to 1 L)	500 g
½ cup	unsalted butter or margarine, softened	125 mL
⅓ cup	milk	75 mL
¼ tsp	almond extract	1 mL

TIP: To melt chocolate in the microwave, use chocolate chips, chocolate squares (each 1 oz/30 g) or small chunks of chocolate. Place in a microwave-safe bowl, cover tightly with plastic wrap and microwave on High for approximately 1 minute per ounce (30 g). (Times will vary depending on the power of your microwave and the quantity of chocolate used.) Remove from microwave and stir until smooth.

VARIATION: Instead of the white fluffy frosting, prepare your favorite chocolate frosting. Dip the tops of each cupcake into the chocolate frosting and sprinkle crushed nuts, grated white chocolate or any other decoration over top.

- *Preheat oven to 375°F (190°C)*
- *12 muffin cups, greased or paper-lined*

1. In a large mixer bowl, cream butter until smooth. Gradually add sugar, beating until fluffy.

2. In a small bowl or cup, beat the egg yolks well. Add to creamed mixture, beating until mixture is light and fluffy.

3. In a medium bowl, sift together flour, baking powder, baking soda and salt. Add to creamed mixture alternately with the milk, stirring only until well blended. Add vanilla and the melted chocolate and mix well.

4. In a small mixer bowl, beat egg whites until stiff peaks form. Fold into batter. Spoon into prepared muffin cups, filling about three-quarters full.

5. Bake in preheated oven for 20 to 25 minutes, or until a toothpick inserted in the center comes out clean and dry. Cool completely on wire rack.

6. *Prepare white fluffy frosting:* In a small mixer bowl, beat confectioner's sugar, butter, milk and almond extract until smooth, about 3 to 5 minutes. Spread onto tops of cupcakes.

Mini Cocoa Cupcakes

MAKES 24 MINI CUPCAKES

1/3 cup	all-purpose flour	75 mL
3 tbsp	unsweetened cocoa powder	45 mL
1/2 tsp	ground cinnamon	2 mL
5	egg whites	5
1/2 tsp	cream of tartar	2 mL
2/3 cup	super-fine granulated sugar	150 mL
Topping		
1/3 cup	semi-sweet chocolate chips (about 2 oz/60 g)	75 mL
3 tbsp	whipping (35%) cream	45 mL

- *Preheat oven to 350°F (180°C)*
- *24 mini muffin cups, greased*

1. In a medium bowl, sift flour, cocoa and cinnamon and mix to blend.
2. In a large mixer bowl, on medium speed, beat egg whites and cream of tartar until frothy. Add sugar, one spoonful at a time, beating for about 5 minutes, until mixture forms glossy, stiff peaks.
3. Fold half of the flour mixture into the egg whites. Gradually fold in the remaining flour mixture until well incorporated. Spoon into prepared muffin cups, using a teaspoon or a melon ball scoop, filling each to the top.
4. Bake in preheated oven for 15 to 20 minutes, or until puffy and a toothpick inserted into the center comes out dry. Cool in pan for 5 minutes and then remove onto wire rack to cool completely.
5. *Prepare topping:* In a small saucepan, over low heat, cook chocolate chips and cream, whisking until melted and smooth. Dip tops of the mini cupcakes into the melted chocolate mixture, then stand upright on a baking sheet or waxed paper.

Chocolate Chip Instant Cupcakes

MAKES 12 CUPCAKES

1	package (18 oz/510 g) yellow cake mix	1
1	package (3 oz/90 g) instant vanilla pudding mix	1
4	eggs	4
1/2 cup	vegetable oil	125 mL
1 cup	mini or regular semi-sweet chocolate chips (about 6 oz/175 g)	250 mL
	Can of prepared frosting (optional)	

- *Preheat oven to 375°F (190°C)*
- *12 muffin cups, greased or paper-lined*

1. In a large mixer bowl, combine cake mix, pudding mix, eggs, 1 cup (250 mL) water and oil and beat on low speed until blended. Continue beating on medium speed for 5 minutes, or until well incorporated.
2. Stir or fold in chocolate chips until well blended. Spoon into prepared muffin cups, filling three-quarters full.
3. Bake in preheated oven for 15 to 20 minutes, or until a toothpick inserted in the center comes out clean and dry. Cool in pan for 10 minutes, then remove onto wire rack to cool completely. Frost with prepared frosting, if desired, or leave plain.

Cream Cheese Chocolate Surprise

MAKES 12 TO 18 CUPCAKES

1½ cups	all-purpose flour	375 mL
1 cup	granulated sugar	250 mL
¼ cup	unsweetened cocoa powder	50 mL
1 tsp	baking soda	5 mL
½ tsp	salt	2 mL
⅓ cup	vegetable oil	75 mL
1 tbsp	vinegar	15 mL
1 tsp	vanilla	5 mL
	Sifted confectioner's (icing) sugar (optional)	

Filling

⅓ cup	granulated sugar	75 mL
1	package (8 oz/250 g) cream cheese, softened	1
1	egg	1
Pinch	salt	Pinch
1 cup	semi-sweet chocolate pieces or chips (about 6 oz/175 g)	250 mL

TIP: You could use a chocolate cake mix with the filling instead.

• *Preheat oven to 350°F (180°C)*
• *12 to 18 muffin cups, greased or paper-lined*

1. In a large bowl, combine flour, sugar, cocoa, baking soda and salt. Mix to blend and make a well in the center.

2. In a small bowl, whisk 1 cup (250 mL) water, oil, vinegar and vanilla. Pour into flour mixture and stir until well blended.

3. *Prepare filling:* In a medium mixer bowl, on medium speed, cream sugar and cream cheese until smooth. Beat in the egg and salt, beating until well incorporated. Stir in chocolate pieces and mix well.

4. Spoon batter into prepared muffin cups, filling only half full. Drop 1 tbsp (15 mL) of the filling over top, then top with remaining batter.

5. Bake in preheated oven for 25 to 30 minutes, or until a toothpick inserted into the center of a cupcake comes out clean and dry. Cool in pan for 10 minutes, then remove onto wire rack to cool completely. Dust tops with confectioner's sugar, if desired.

Chocolate Volcano Cupcakes

MAKES 8 CUPCAKES

1 cup	all-purpose flour	250 mL
¼ tsp	salt	1 mL
1 cup	butter, softened	250 mL
½ cup	granulated sugar	125 mL
3	eggs	3
3	egg yolks	3
1 tsp	vanilla	5 mL
2 cups	semi-sweet chocolate chips, melted (about 12 oz/375 g)	500 mL
1 cup	ground pecans, toasted (optional)	250 mL
4	squares (each 1 oz/30 g) white baking chocolate, cut into 8 pieces	4
	Sifted confectioner's (icing) sugar (optional)	

- *Preheat oven to 350°F (180°C)*
- *Eight ¾-cup (175 mL) custard cups, greased and placed on a baking sheet*

1. In a small bowl, mix together flour and salt.
2. In a large mixer bowl, cream butter and sugar until smooth. Add eggs, egg yolks and vanilla, beating on low speed. Beat in melted chocolate until well blended.
3. Add flour mixture to creamed mixture and stir in pecans, if using. Spoon into prepared custard cups and bake in preheated oven for 10 minutes.
4. Remove from oven and push one piece of the white chocolate into the center of each cupcake. Return to oven and bake for another 15 to 20 minutes longer, or until a toothpick inserted into a cupcake comes out clean and dry.
5. Remove from oven and let stand in cups for about 5 minutes. Run a knife around the edges of the custard cups and slowly invert each custard cup onto individual serving plates. Sprinkle some confectioner's sugar over tops, if desired.

Coconut Cupcakes

MAKES 24 CUPCAKES

2¼ cups	sifted cake flour	550 mL
1½ cups	granulated sugar, divided	375 mL
3 tsp	baking powder	15 mL
1 tsp	salt	5 mL
1 cup	milk, divided	250 mL
⅓ cup	vegetable oil	75 mL
1½ tsp	vanilla	7 mL
2	eggs, separated	2
1⅓ cups	flaked coconut	325 mL
	Can of prepared frosting	

- *Preheat oven to 400°F (200°C)*
- *24 muffin cups, greased or paper-lined*

1. In a large mixer bowl, sift together cake flour, 1 cup (250 mL) of the sugar, baking powder and salt. Mix well.

2. In a small bowl, combine ½ cup (125 mL) of the milk, oil and vanilla. Pour into flour mixture and stir with a spoon until blended. Then beat on medium speed for about 2 minutes, scraping sides of bowl. Add the remaining ½ cup (125 mL) milk and the egg yolks and beat for another 2 minutes.

3. In a small mixer bowl, beat egg whites until soft peaks form. Gradually add the remaining ½ cup (125 mL) sugar, beating until stiff peaks form. Gently fold into batter.

4. Spoon into prepared muffin cups, filling about three-quarters full. Top with the coconut. Bake in preheated oven for 12 to 15 minutes, or until a toothpick inserted in the center comes out clean and dry. Frost with a creamy frosting, such as cream cheese frosting.

Cocoa-Cola Cupcakes

MAKES 12 CUPCAKES

2 cups	all-purpose flour	500 mL
1¼ cups	granulated sugar	300 mL
½ cup	unsweetened cocoa powder	125 mL
½ tsp	salt	2 mL
½ tsp	baking soda	2 mL
⅔ cup	milk	150 mL
½ cup	vegetable oil	125 mL
3	eggs	3
½ tsp	vanilla	2 mL
1	bottle or can (12 oz/355 mL) cola	1

- *Preheat oven to 350°F (180°C)*
- *12 muffin cups, greased or paper-lined*

1. In a large bowl, combine flour, sugar, cocoa, salt and baking soda. Mix well to blend. Make a well in the center.

2. In a small bowl, whisk milk, oil, eggs and vanilla. Add cola and whisk until blended. Pour into flour mixture and mix until well incorporated. Spoon into prepared muffin cups.

3. Bake in preheated oven for 30 to 35 minutes, or until a toothpick inserted into the center of a cupcake comes out clean and dry. Cool on wire rack.

Cupcake Cones

MAKES 24 CUPCAKE CONES

2 cups	all-purpose flour	500 mL
2½ tsp	baking powder	12 mL
½ tsp	salt	2 mL
1½ cups	firmly packed brown sugar	375 mL
⅓ cup	butter or margarine, softened	75 mL
½ cup	creamy peanut butter, at room temperature	125 mL
1 tsp	vanilla	5 mL
2	eggs	2
	White frosting	
½ cup	chopped peanuts or sprinkles	125 mL

- *Preheat oven to 350°F (180°C)*
- *24 flat-bottom ice cream cones, placed in muffin cups*

1. In a large bowl, combine flour, baking powder and salt and mix well.
2. In a large mixer bowl, cream together brown sugar, butter and peanut butter until smooth. Beat in vanilla and then eggs. Add to flour mixture alternately with the milk, beating only until well incorporated. Spoon about 3 tbsp (45 mL) of the batter into each cone, leaving about ½ inch (1 cm) at the top of each cone.
3. Bake in preheated oven for 30 minutes, or until a toothpick inserted in the center of a cupcake comes out clean and dry. Leave cones in pan for 10 minutes, then remove onto wire rack to cool completely.
4. Frost with a favorite white frosting and sprinkle peanuts or sprinkles over tops.

Creamy Cookie Cupcakes

MAKES 24 CUPCAKES

1	package (18 oz/510 g) white cake mix	1
⅓ cup	vegetable oil	75 mL
3	eggs, lightly beaten	3
10	cream-filled sandwich cookies, either vanilla or chocolate, cut into ¼-inch (0.5 cm) chunks	10
Frosting		
2 tbsp	butter or margarine	25 mL
2	squares (each 1 oz/30 g) unsweetened chocolate, chopped	2
1 cup	sifted confectioner's (icing) sugar	250 mL
¼ cup	milk	50 mL

- *Preheat oven to 350°F (180°C)*
- *24 muffin cups, greased or paper-lined*

1. Prepare cake mix according to directions on package, but mix with the oil and eggs. Add cookie chunks and stir until well incorporated.
2. Bake in preheated oven according to cupcake directions on package, but check cupcakes about 10 minutes before the suggested time. Cool in cups for 10 minutes and then remove onto wire rack and cool completely.
3. *Prepare frosting:* In a small saucepan, over low heat, melt the butter and chocolate. Set aside to cool. Gradually whisk in confectioner's sugar until well blended. Beat in just enough milk until mixture is of an icing consistency. Spread over tops of cupcakes.

Frozen Fruit Cupcakes

MAKES 18 CUPCAKES

1	can (10 oz/284 mL) mandarin orange segments, drained	1
1	jar (12 oz/375 mL) maraschino cherries, drained	1
½ cup	granulated sugar	125 mL
1	package (8 oz/250 g) cream cheese, softened	1
1	can (8 oz/227 mL) crushed pineapple, drained	1
½ cup	chopped nuts (pecans or other)	125 mL
1 cup	frozen whipped topping, thawed (about 8 oz/250 g)	250 mL

- *18 muffin cups, paper-lined*

1. Set aside 18 orange segments and 9 halved cherries, then chop the remaining cherries.
2. In a large mixer bowl, on medium speed, cream sugar and cream cheese until smooth and fluffy. Add the pineapple, pecans and chopped cherries and mix until well incorporated. Fold in the whipped topping and the remaining orange segments.
3. Spoon mixture into the prepared muffin cups. Top each with a reserved cherry half and orange segment. Freeze in freezer until firm. Remove from freezer about 10 minutes before serving.

Fudge Nut Cupcakes

MAKES 18 TO 24 CUPCAKES

1⅓ cups	sifted all-purpose flour	325 mL
1 tsp	baking soda	5 mL
½ tsp	salt	2 mL
2	squares (each 1 oz/30 g) unsweetened chocolate	2
1⅓ cup	lightly packed brown sugar, divided	325 mL
⅓ cup	milk	75 mL
⅓ cup	butter, or shortening, softened	75 mL
1 tsp	vanilla	5 mL
2	eggs	2
½ cup	milk	125 mL
½ cup	chopped nuts	125 mL

- *Preheat oven to 375°F (190°C)*
- *18 to 24 muffin cups, greased or paper-lined*

1. In a medium bowl, sift together flour, baking soda and salt.
2. In a small saucepan, over low heat, cook chocolate, ⅔ cup (150 mL) of the brown sugar and the ⅓ cup (75 mL) milk, stirring until chocolate melts. Set aside to cool.
3. In a large mixer bowl, cream the remaining ⅔ cup (150 mL) brown sugar, butter and vanilla until light and fluffy. Beat in eggs, one at a time, beating well after each addition. Add flour mixture alternately with the ½ cup (125 mL) of milk, beating well after each addition. Stir in chocolate mixture and then the nuts until well incorporated.
4. Spoon into prepared muffin cups, filling three-quarters full, and bake in preheated oven for 15 to 20 minutes, or until a toothpick inserted in the center of a cupcake comes out clean and dry. Cool for 10 minutes in pan, remove and place on wire rack to cool completely.

Frosted Fudgey Cocoa Cupcakes

MAKES 20 CUPCAKES

1 ¼ cups	all-purpose flour	300 mL
¾ cup	unsweetened cocoa powder	175 mL
3 tsp	baking powder	15 mL
½ tsp	salt	2 mL
1 ¼ cups	granulated sugar	300 mL
½ cup	butter or margarine, softened	125 mL
3	eggs	3
1 tsp	vanilla	5 mL
⅔ cup	milk	150 mL

Fudgey Frosting

⅓ cup	butter or margarine	75 mL
⅓ cup	unsweetened cocoa powder	75 mL
½ tsp	vanilla	2 mL
3 cups	sifted confectioner's (icing) sugar	750 mL
¼ cup	milk	50 mL

- *Preheat oven to 375°F (190°C)*
- *20 muffin cups, paper-lined*

1. Sift together flour, cocoa, baking powder and salt.

2. In a large mixer bowl, cream sugar and butter until smooth. Beat in eggs one at a time, beating well after each addition. Add vanilla. Add the cocoa mixture alternately with the milk and blend on low speed, combining lightly after each addition.

3. Spoon into prepared muffin cups evenly and bake in preheated oven for 20 to 25 minutes, or until a toothpick inserted in the center of a cupcake comes out clean and dry. Cool completely on wire rack.

4. *Prepare fudgey frosting:* In a small saucepan, melt the butter. Remove from heat and stir in the cocoa and vanilla. Stir in the confectioner's sugar alternately with the milk, stirring only until frosting is smooth and of spreading consistency. Spread frosting on tops of cooled cupcakes and decorate further if desired.

Grandma's Lemon Cupcakes

MAKES 24 TO 30 CUPCAKES

3½ cups	all-purpose flour	875 mL
2 tsp	baking powder	10 mL
1 tsp	baking soda	5 mL
½ tsp	salt	2 mL
1¾ cups	granulated sugar	425 mL
1 cup	butter or margarine, softened	250 mL
1 tsp	vanilla	5 mL
3	eggs	3
2 tsp	grated lemon zest	10 mL
2 cups	sour cream	500 mL

- *Preheat oven to 350°F (180°C)*
- *24 to 30 muffin cups, greased or paper-lined*

1. In a medium bowl, mix together flour, baking powder, baking soda and salt until blended.

2. In a large mixer bowl, on medium-high speed, cream sugar, butter and vanilla until smooth and fluffy. Add eggs one at a time, beating well after each addition. Add lemon zest and mix well.

3. Add flour mixture to creamed mixture alternately with the sour cream, beating until well incorporated and blended. Spoon into prepared muffin cups, filling about three-quarters full.

4. Bake in preheated oven for 25 to 30 minutes, or until a toothpick inserted in the center of a cupcake comes out clean and dry. Cool in pan for 5 to 10 minutes, then remove onto wire rack and cool completely.

Spicy Cupcakes

MAKES 12 CUPCAKES

¼ cup	granulated sugar	50 mL
¼ cup	shortening or butter, softened	50 mL
1	egg	1
½ cup	unsulphured molasses	125 mL
½ cup	boiling water	125 mL
1¼ cups	all-purpose flour	300 mL
1 tsp	baking soda	5 mL
1 tsp	ground cinnamon	5 mL
½ tsp	ground nutmeg	2 mL
¼ tsp	ground cloves	1 mL
Pinch	salt	Pinch

- *Preheat oven to 350°F (180°C)*
- *12 muffin cups, greased or paper-lined*

1. In a large mixer bowl, cream sugar and shortening. Add egg and beat until smooth and blended.

2. In a small bowl, mix together molasses and water.

3. In a medium bowl, combine flour, baking soda, cinnamon, nutmeg, cloves and salt. Mix together to blend. Add flour mixture to the creamed mixture alternately with the molasses mixture, beating well after each addition. Spoon into prepared muffin cups, filling about three-quarters full.

4. Bake in preheated oven for 18 to 20 minutes, or until a toothpick inserted in the center of a cupcake comes out clean and dry. Cool in pan for 5 minutes, then remove onto wire rack to cool completely.

Traditional Vanilla Cupcakes

MAKES 12 CUPCAKES

½ cup	butter (no substitute), softened	125 mL
2	eggs	2
½ cup	milk	125 mL
1 tsp	vanilla	5 mL
2 cups	sifted cake flour	500 mL
¾ cup	granulated sugar	175 mL
2 tsp	baking powder	10 mL
½ tsp	salt	2 mL

TIP: Because the cupcakes are a neutral vanilla, you can use any type of frosting — even a vanilla frosting with a few drops of food coloring. Or make a rainbow of cupcakes with different colors of frosting.

- *Preheat oven to 375°F (190°C)*
- *12 muffin cups, paper-lined*

1. In a large mixer bowl, cream butter and eggs. Add milk and vanilla and beat on low speed until blended.
2. In a medium bowl, sift together cake flour, sugar, baking powder and salt. Add to creamed mixture and beat on medium speed until smooth and well blended. Spoon into prepared muffin cups, filling about three-quarters full.
3. Bake in preheated oven for 15 to 20 minutes, or until a toothpick inserted in the center of a cupcake comes out clean and dry. Cool in pan for 10 minutes, then remove and place on wire rack to cool completely.

Peanut Butter 'n' Jelly Cupcakes

MAKES 24 CUPCAKES

2 cups	all-purpose flour	500 mL
2 tsp	baking powder	10 mL
½ tsp	salt	2 mL
½ cup	peanut butter, at room temperature	125 mL
⅓ cup	butter or shortening, softened	75 mL
1 tsp	vanilla	5 mL
1½ cups	firmly packed brown sugar	375 mL
2	eggs	2
¾ cup	milk	175 mL
½ cup	jelly or jam (your favorite)	125 mL

- *Preheat oven to 375°F (190°C)*
- *24 muffin cups, paper-lined*

1. In a medium bowl, mix together flour, baking powder and salt until blended.
2. In a large mixer bowl, on medium speed, beat peanut butter, butter and vanilla until smooth. Gradually add brown sugar, beating until light and fluffy. Add eggs one at a time, beating after each addition.
3. Add flour mixture to creamed mixture alternately with the milk, mixing well. Spoon batter into prepared muffin cups, filling about half full. Drop a teaspoonful of the jelly into the center of each cup and top with remaining batter.
4. Bake in preheated oven for 20 to 25 minutes, or until a toothpick inserted into the center of a cupcake comes out clean and dry. Remove from pan immediately and cool completely on wire rack.

Pumpkin Cupcakes with Lemon Cream Cheese Frosting

MAKES 12 CUPCAKES

1¼ cups	granulated sugar	300 mL
1¼ cups	canned pumpkin purée (or cooked, puréed and cooled)	300 mL
½ cup	vegetable oil	125 mL
2	eggs	2
1⅓ cups	all-purpose flour	325 mL
2 tsp	ground cinnamon	10 mL
1½ tsp	baking powder	7 mL
½ tsp	baking soda	2 mL
½ tsp	salt	2 mL
½ tsp	ground ginger	2 mL

Lemon Cream Cheese Frosting

1	package (8 oz/250 g) cream cheese, softened	1
1 cup	sifted confectioner's (icing) sugar	250 mL
	Finely grated zest of 1 lemon	
2 to 3 tbsp	freshly squeezed lemon juice	25 to 45 mL

- *Preheat oven to 350°F (180°C)*
- *12 muffin cups, greased or paper-lined*

1. In a large bowl, whisk together sugar, pumpkin, oil and eggs until well blended.

2. In a small bowl, mix together flour, cinnamon, baking powder, baking soda, salt and ginger. Add flour mixture to pumpkin mixture and mix well. Spoon into prepared muffin cups, filling about three-quarters full.

3. Bake in preheated oven for 18 to 20 minutes, or until a toothpick inserted in the center of a cupcake comes out clean and dry. Cool in pan for 10 minutes, then remove onto wire rack to cool completely.

4. *Prepare lemon cream cheese frosting:* In a small mixer bowl, beat cream cheese and confectioner's sugar until smooth. Add lemon zest and juice and continue to beat until smooth and blended. Swirl the tops of each cupcake with frosting.

Rice Cupcakes

2	eggs	2
¼ cup	packed brown sugar	50 mL
1 cup	cooked white rice	250 mL
1 cup	all-purpose flour	250 mL
3 tsp	baking powder	15 mL
¼ tsp	salt	1 mL
¾ cup	milk	175 mL
2 tbsp	butter or margarine, melted	25 mL
½ tsp	vanilla	2 mL

- *Preheat oven to 400°F (200°C)*
- *14 to 16 muffin cups, greased or paper-lined*

1. In a large mixer bowl, beat eggs. Add brown sugar and beat well.
2. Stir in the rice and mix to blend.
3. In a small bowl, combine flour, baking powder and salt. Stir into egg and rice mixture, mixing until well blended. Add the melted butter and vanilla and beat until well combined. Spoon into prepared muffin cups, filling about three-quarters full.
4. Bake in preheated oven for 25 to 30 minutes, or until a toothpick inserted in the center of a cupcake comes out clean and dry. Cool on wire rack.

Caramel Zucchini Cupcakes

2½ cups	all-purpose flour	625 mL
2 tsp	baking powder	10 mL
2 tsp	ground cinnamon	10 mL
1 tsp	salt	5 mL
1 tsp	baking soda	5 mL
½ tsp	ground cloves	2 mL
1¼ cups	granulated sugar	300 mL
½ cup	vegetable oil	125 mL
½ cup	freshly squeezed orange juice	125 mL
3	eggs	3
1 tsp	almond extract	5 mL
1½ cups	shredded zucchini	375 mL

Caramel Frosting

1 cup	firmly packed brown sugar	250 mL
½ cup	butter or margarine	125 mL
¼ cup	milk	50 mL
1 tsp	vanilla	5 mL
1¾ cups	sifted confectioner's (icing) sugar	425 mL

- *Preheat oven to 350°F (180°C)*
- *20 to 24 muffin cups, greased or paper-lined*

1. In a medium bowl, combine flour, baking powder, cinnamon, salt, baking soda and cloves. Whisk together until well blended.
2. In a large mixer bowl, on medium speed, combine sugar, oil, orange juice, eggs and almond extract, beating just to blend.
3. Add the flour mixture to the egg mixture and mix until well incorporated. Add zucchini and mix well. Spoon into prepared muffin cups, filling about three-quarters full.
4. Bake in preheated oven for 20 to 25 minutes, or until a toothpick inserted in the center of a cupcake comes out clean and dry. Cool in pan for 10 minutes, then remove onto wire rack to cool completely.
5. *Prepare caramel frosting:* In a medium saucepan, over medium heat, combine brown sugar, butter and milk and bring to a boil, stirring for 2 minutes. Remove from heat, add vanilla, mix well and cool until lukewarm. Whisk in the confectioner's sugar, beating until mixture is of the right spreading consistency. Spread over tops of cupcakes.

Cobblers

Apple Cinnamon Cobbler

SERVES 6

1 cup	granulated sugar	250 mL
2 tbsp	all-purpose flour	25 mL
1 tsp	ground cinnamon	5 mL
1/4 tsp	ground nutmeg	1 mL
6 cups	peeled, sliced, tart apples (about 6 medium)	1.5 L

Biscuit Topping

1 cup	all-purpose flour	250 mL
2 tbsp	granulated sugar	25 mL
1 1/2 tsp	baking powder	7 mL
1/4 tsp	salt	1 mL
1/4 cup	shortening or butter	50 mL
1	egg, lightly beaten	1
1/4 cup	milk	50 mL
1/2 tsp	vanilla	2 mL

- *Preheat oven to 400°F (200°C)*
- *8-inch (20 cm) round cake pan, lightly greased*

1. In a large saucepan, over medium heat, combine sugar, flour, cinnamon and nutmeg until well blended. Add apples and toss until well blended and coated. Cook, stirring, until apples are almost tender, about 7 to 8 minutes. Spoon apple mixture into prepared cake pan.

2. *Prepare biscuit topping:* In a large bowl, combine flour, sugar, baking powder and salt. Cut in shortening until mixture resembles coarse crumbs. Add egg, milk and vanilla and mix well to blend.

3. Drop mounds or spoonfuls of this dough onto apple mixture and bake in preheated oven for 20 to 25 minutes, or until topping is golden brown. Cool slightly and serve warm.

Cran-Apple Cobbler

SERVES 6

4 1/2 cups	peeled, cored, coarsely chopped cooking apples (about 4 1/2 medium)	1.125 L
1 1/2 cups	fresh or frozen cranberries (about 6 oz/175 g)	375 mL
1/2 cup	granulated sugar	125 mL
2 tbsp	flour	25 mL
1 tsp	grated orange zest (optional)	5 mL
3/4 cup	freshly squeezed orange juice	175 mL

Topping

3/4 cup	all-purpose flour	175 mL
2 tbsp	granulated sugar	25 mL
1 tsp	baking powder	5 mL
Pinch	salt	Pinch
1/4 cup	cold butter or margarine	50 mL
1/4 cup	milk	50 mL

- *Preheat oven to 375°F (190°C)*
- *9-inch (23 cm) round cake pan or pie plate, greased*

1. In a large saucepan, combine apples, cranberries, sugar, flour, orange zest (if desired) and orange juice. Bring to a boil, then reduce heat, cover and simmer for about 3 minutes, stirring, until apples are nearly tender. Spoon into prepared baking pan and set aside.

2. *Prepare topping:* In a medium bowl, mix together flour, sugar, baking powder and salt. Cut in the butter with a pastry blender or two knives until mixture is crumbly. Add milk and stir until a soft dough forms. Drop dough by spoonfuls over the hot apple mixture.

3. Bake, uncovered, in preheated oven for 35 minutes, or until topping is golden brown. Delicious when served warm.

Cobbler Cake with Applesauce

SERVES 6 TO 8

2 cups	sifted all-purpose flour	500 mL
¼ cup	granulated sugar	50 mL
3 tsp	baking powder	15 mL
1 tsp	salt	5 mL
⅓ cup	cold butter or shortening	75 mL
1	egg	1
½ cup	milk	125 mL

Applesauce

⅓ cup + 1 tbsp	butter or margarine	90 mL
⅓ cup	firmly packed brown sugar	75 mL
½ cup	sweetened applesauce	125 mL
1 tbsp	corn syrup	15 mL
¾ tsp	ground cinnamon	4 mL

- *Preheat oven to 400°F (200°C)*
- *9-inch (23 cm) round cake pan, greased*

1. In a large bowl, sift together flour, sugar, baking powder and salt. Cut in the butter with a pastry blender, or crumble with your hands, until mixture resembles coarse crumbs.

2. In a small bowl, combine egg and milk and beat until blended. Pour into flour mixture and stir only until blended. Do not over-mix.

3. *Prepare applesauce:* In a small bowl, cream butter and brown sugar until light and smooth. Stir in applesauce, corn syrup and cinnamon and mix well.

4. Drop cake mixture by spoonfuls into prepared cake pan. Spoon the applesauce mixture over dough and bake in preheated oven for 30 to 35 minutes, or until the cake pulls away from the side of the pan. Cut into wedges and serve warm.

Apricot Cobbler

SERVES 6

¾ cup	granulated sugar	175 mL
1 tbsp	cornstarch	15 mL
½ tsp	ground cinnamon	2 mL
Pinch	ground nutmeg	Pinch
1 tbsp	butter or margarine	15 mL
3	cans (each 15 oz/425 mL) apricot halves, drained	3

Biscuit Topping

1 cup	all-purpose flour	250 mL
4 tsp	granulated sugar	20 mL
1½ tsp	baking powder	7 mL
½ tsp	salt	2 mL
2 tbsp	shortening or butter	25 mL
⅓ cup	milk	75 mL

- *Preheat oven to 400°F (200°C)*
- *11- by 7-inch (2 L) baking dish, greased*

1. In a large saucepan, mix together sugar, cornstarch, cinnamon and nutmeg. Add 1 cup (250 mL) water and bring to a boil over medium heat. Boil, stirring, for about 1 minute, then reduce the heat. Add butter and apricots, stirring just until heated through. Spoon into prepared baking dish.

2. *Prepare biscuit topping:* In a medium bowl, mix together flour, sugar, baking powder and salt. Cut in shortening with a pastry blender or two knives until mixture is crumbly. Stir in milk, just until moistened. Drop by spoonfuls over apricot mixture.

3. Bake in preheated oven for 30 to 35 minutes, or until topping is golden brown and a toothpick inserted into the topping comes out clean and dry. Serve warm or at room temperature.

Fresh Blueberry Cobbler

SERVES 6 TO 8

Dough

1 cup	all-purpose flour	250 mL
½ cup	granulated sugar	125 mL
1 tsp	baking powder	5 mL
¼ tsp	salt	1 mL
1	egg	1
¼ cup	butter or margarine, melted	50 mL
¼ cup	milk	50 mL
1 tsp	vanilla	5 mL

Blueberry Topping

3 cups	fresh blueberries (about 1 lb/500 g)	750 mL
¼ cup	granulated sugar	50 mL
½ tsp	ground cinnamon	2 mL
1 tsp	freshly squeezed lemon juice (optional)	5 mL
1 tbsp	butter or margarine	15 mL

- *Preheat oven to 350°F (180°C)*
- *9- or 10-inch (23 or 25 cm) pie plate, lightly greased*

1. *Prepare dough:* In a large bowl, combine flour, sugar, baking powder and salt and mix until well blended. Make a well in the center.
2. In a small bowl, whisk egg, melted butter, milk and vanilla. Pour into the flour mixture, stirring only until blended and moistened, as for a pie dough. Spoon into prepared pie dish and spread evenly to cover bottom.
3. *Prepare blueberry topping:* In a large bowl, toss blueberries, sugar, cinnamon and lemon juice, if using, until well mixed. Spread over dough and dot with the butter.
4. Bake in preheated oven for 45 to 50 minutes, or until juice bubbles up. Best when served warm.

Quick 'n' Easy Blueberry Cobbler

SERVES 6

1	package (14 oz/400 g) blueberry muffin mix	1
1	can (19 oz/540 mL) blueberry pie filling	1
1 tbsp	freshly squeezed lemon juice	15 mL
1 tsp	ground cinnamon	5 mL

- *Preheat oven to 400°F (200°C)*
- *9-inch (2.5 L) square baking pan, ungreased*

1. Open the can of blueberries that comes in the muffin mix package and drain, setting aside the liquid.
2. In a small saucepan, combine the reserved liquid, pie filling, lemon juice and cinnamon and heat to boiling. Remove from stove and pour into baking pan.
3. Prepare the muffin mix as directed on the package, but pour the finished batter onto the hot pie filling mixture, spreading evenly, or drop muffin mixture by spoonfuls onto hot filling.
4. Bake in preheated oven for 25 to 30 minutes, or until top is golden brown. Serve warm or at room temperature.

Old-Fashioned Cherry Cobbler

SERVES 6

6 cups	stemmed and pitted sweet or sour cherries	1.5 L
1 cup	granulated sugar	250 mL
1/4 cup	cornstarch	50 mL
2 tbsp	freshly squeezed orange juice or cherry brandy	25 mL
2 tsp	freshly squeezed lemon juice	10 mL

Topping

1 cup	all-purpose flour	250 mL
1 1/2 tsp	baking powder	7 mL
1/4 tsp	salt	1 mL
1/4 cup	cold butter or shortening, cut into pieces	50 mL
1/3 cup	milk	75 mL
1 tsp	vanilla	5 mL

TIP: If using frozen cherries, thaw and drain well before combining with the other ingredients.

VARIATION: For a delightful addition, mix together about 1/3 to 1/2 cup (75 to 125 mL) of blanched sliced almonds and 2 tsp (10 mL) of granulated sugar and sprinkle over dough before baking.

- *Preheat oven to 400°F (200°C)*
- *9-inch (2.5 L) square baking dish, ungreased*

1. Place cherries in a large bowl.
2. In a small bowl, mix together sugar and cornstarch. Stir in orange juice and lemon juice. Pour into bowl of cherries and stir until well mixed. Place mixture into baking dish.
3. *Prepare topping:* In another small bowl, mix together flour, baking powder and salt. Cut in butter, using a pastry blender or two knives, until mixture is crumbly. Add milk and vanilla and mix just until you have a thick dough.
4. Drop the dough by spoonfuls onto the fruit mixture and, with the back of a spoon, smooth out dough until even and touching the sides of the pan.
5. Bake in preheated oven for 25 to 30 minutes, or until fruit filling is bubbling and the top is golden brown. Let stand for 10 to 15 minutes before serving.

Chocolate Nut Cobbler

SERVES 6 TO 8

5 to 6 tbsp	butter or margarine	75 to 90 mL
1½ cups	granulated sugar, divided	375 mL
1 cup	self-rising flour	250 mL
½ cup	chopped nuts (pecans, almonds or other)	125 mL
½ cup	milk	125 mL
⅓ cup	unsweetened cocoa powder, divided	75 mL
1 tsp	vanilla	5 mL
1½ cups	boiling water	375 mL
	Fudge sundae topping	

- *Preheat oven to 350°F (180°C)*
- *13- by 9-inch (3 L) baking dish*

1. Melt the butter in the baking dish in preheated oven. Remove from oven when melted.

2. In a large bowl, mix together ½ cup (125 mL) of the granulated sugar, flour, nuts, milk, 2 tbsp (25 mL) of the cocoa and vanilla, mixing until well blended. Spoon mixture into baking dish over the melted butter. Do not stir or mix.

3. In a small bowl, mix together the remaining 1 cup (250 mL) of sugar and the remaining ¼ cup (50 mL) of cocoa and sprinkle this mixture over the batter. Again do not stir or mix.

4. Pour the boiling water over top; again do not stir or mix. Bake in preheated oven for 25 to 30 minutes, or until golden brown. Set aside to cool slightly, just until warm. When serving, spoon some fudge sundae topping over top.

Canned Fruit Cookie Cobbler

SERVES 6

1	can (19 oz/540 mL) fruit, such as raspberries, sliced peaches or sweetened cherries, drained, reserve liquid	1
1 tbsp	butter or margarine	15 mL
1 cup	reserved canned fruit syrup	250 mL
2 tbsp	all-purpose flour	25 mL
1	roll (18 oz/510 g) prepared sugar cookie dough	1

- *Preheat oven to 375°F (190°C)*
- *6-cup (1.5 L) casserole dish, ungreased*

1. Spoon drained fruit into casserole dish.

2. In a small saucepan, melt the butter. Stir in syrup and flour and cook over low heat until mixture thickens. Pour thickened mixture over the fruit.

3. Crumble cookie dough over fruit, covering thickly and completely.

4. Bake, uncovered, in preheated oven for 20 to 25 minutes, or until juices are bubbly and the cookie crust is golden brown and crisp.

Jiffy Cobbler

SERVES 6 TO 8

2	cans (each 19 oz/540 mL) prepared peach pie filling	2
2 cups	fresh blueberries (about 12 oz/375 g) (optional)	500 mL
1	package (18 oz/510 g) yellow cake mix	1
½ cup	butter or margarine, melted	125 mL
½ cup	chopped nuts (pecans, almonds, or walnuts)	125 mL

VARIATIONS

Use apple pie filling and spice cake mix.

Use blueberry pie filling and lemon cake mix.

Use cherry pie filling and chocolate cake mix.

Use any pie filling you may have on hand and combine with any cake mix on hand.

You can also add other berries or fruits, mixed with the pie filling.

- *Preheat oven to 350°F (180°C)*
- *8-inch (2 L) square baking pan, lightly greased*

1. In a large bowl, mix together peach pie filling and blueberries (if using) and spoon onto bottom of prepared baking pan. Sprinkle cake mix over fruit.
2. Drizzle melted butter over cake mix and sprinkle chopped nuts over top.
3. Bake in preheated oven for 45 to 50 minutes, or until top is golden brown.

Orange Marmalade Cobbler

SERVES 2 TO 3

¼ cup	orange marmalade	50 mL
2 tbsp	frozen orange juice concentrate	25 mL
2 tbsp	granulated sugar	25 mL
1 tbsp	cornstarch	15 mL
2 tsp	butter or margarine	10 mL
½ cup	biscuit mix	125 mL
Pinch	ground nutmeg	Pinch
3 tbsp	milk	45 mL

TIP: If you don't have a 4-cup (1 L) casserole dish, you can use a 6-cup (1.5 L) casserole dish instead.

- *Preheat oven to 400°F (200°C)*
- *4-cup (1 L) casserole dish, greased*

1. In a small saucepan, over medium heat, combine ½ cup (125 mL) cold water, marmalade and orange juice concentrate. Stir in sugar and cornstarch and stir until thickened. Add butter and stir until butter is melted. Pour into prepared casserole dish.
2. In a small bowl, combine biscuit mix and nutmeg. Add milk, stirring just until blended and moistened. Drop by spoonfuls over orange mixture.
3. Bake in preheated oven for 20 to 25 minutes, or until top is golden brown. Best when served warm.

Saucy Nectarine Cobbler

SERVES 6 TO 8

Dough

2 cups	all-purpose flour	500 mL
¼ tsp	salt	1 mL
½ cup	shortening, chilled	125 mL
⅓ cup	ice water	75 mL

Filling

8	fresh nectarines	8
¾ to 1 cup	granulated sugar	175 to 250 mL
¼ cup	cornstarch (optional)	50 mL
¼ cup	butter or margarine	50 mL

Sauce (optional)

⅔ cup	granulated sugar	150 mL
2 tsp	cornstarch	10 mL
½ tsp	ground nutmeg	2 mL
¼ tsp	ground cinnamon (optional)	1 mL
Pinch	salt	Pinch
3 tbsp to ¼ cup	peach-flavored brandy (optional)	45 to 50 mL

- 8-inch (2 L) square baking dish, ungreased

1. *Prepare dough:* In a medium bowl, mix together flour and salt. Cut in shortening with a pastry blender or two knives until mixture is crumbly. Add the ice water and mix until a ball of dough is formed that holds together. Wrap in plastic wrap and chill in refrigerator for 3 to 4 hours or overnight.

2. Set aside one-quarter of the dough and roll out remaining dough to fit the bottom and sides of baking dish. Preheat oven to 425°F (220°C).

3. *Prepare filling:* Slice nectarines and place in a large bowl with sugar and cornstarch. Toss until well combined. Spoon fruit mixture into pastry-lined pan. Dot with butter.

4. Roll out the reserved dough, cut into strips and place on fruit in a lattice pattern, sealing edges. Bake in preheated oven for 35 to 40 minutes, or until filling is bubbly and top crust is lightly browned.

5. *If desired, prepare sauce:* In a small saucepan, over medium heat, bring 1 cup (250 mL) water to a boil. Stir in sugar, cornstarch, nutmeg, cinnamon and salt and bring back to a boil, stirring constantly. Cook until thickened and then remove from heat. Add brandy, if desired.

6. Serve cobbler warm, Drizzle warm sauce, if using, over top.

Individual Peach Cobblers

SERVES 4

1 tbsp	cornstarch	15 mL
1	can (14 oz/398 mL) sliced peaches, with juice	2
¼ tsp	ground cinnamon	1 mL
Topping		
1 cup	biscuit mix	250 mL
4 tsp	granulated sugar	20 mL
¼ cup	milk	50 mL
2 tbsp	vegetable oil	25 mL

TIP: Serve warm with ice cream or whipped cream.

- *Preheat oven to 400°F (200°C)*
- *Four ¾-cup (175 mL) custard cups, buttered*

1. In a medium saucepan, mix together 2 tbsp (25 mL) cold water and cornstarch until smooth. Add the peaches and bring to a boil, stirring over medium heat, until mixture becomes thickened, about 2 to 3 minutes. Spoon into prepared custard cups.

2. *Prepare topping:* In a medium bowl, mix together biscuit mix and sugar until blended. Add milk and oil, stirring just until moistened and blended. Drop by small spoonfuls over each hot peach filling, then sprinkle with cinnamon.

3. Bake in preheated oven for 20 to 25 minutes, or until filling is bubbly and topping is golden brown.

Lazy Day Peach Cobbler

SERVES 4 TO 6

1	package (14 oz/400 g) oatmeal muffin mix	1
¼ tsp	ground nutmeg	1 mL
½ tsp	ground cinnamon (optional)	2 mL
½ cup	butter or margarine	125 mL
Filling		
4 cups	peeled and sliced fresh peaches (about 6 medium)	1 L
¾ cup	granulated sugar	175 mL
2 tbsp	freshly squeezed lemon juice	25 mL

TIP: Serve warm or cool, topped with ice cream or whipped topping.

- *Preheat oven to 375°F (190°C)*
- *8-inch (2 L) square baking dish, ungreased*

1. In a medium bowl, mix together oatmeal mix, nutmeg and cinnamon, if using. Cut in the butter with a pastry blender or two knives until mixture resembles coarse crumbs. Set aside.

2. *Prepare filling:* In a large bowl, combine peaches, sugar and lemon juice. Mix well and spoon into prepared baking dish.

3. Spoon crumbly mixture over peach mixture. Bake in preheated oven for 40 to 50 minutes, or until topping is golden brown.

Skillet Peach Cobbler

SERVES 4 TO 6

2	cans (each 14 oz/398 mL) sliced peaches, with juice	2
3 tbsp	cornstarch	45 mL
3 tbsp	brown sugar	45 mL
2 tbsp	butter or margarine	25 mL
1/2 tsp	ground ginger	2 mL
Dumplings		
1 cup	biscuit mix	250 mL
1/3 cup	milk	75 mL
1 tbsp	brown sugar	15 mL

TIP: Serve warm with whipped topping or ice cream.

1. In a skillet, combine peaches, cornstarch, brown sugar, butter and ginger. Cook over low heat until mixture becomes thickened.
2. *Prepare dumplings:* In a medium bowl, mix together biscuit mix, milk and brown sugar until well blended.
3. Drop by spoonfuls onto bubbly peach mixture and cook, uncovered, for about 10 to 12 minutes. Cover and continue cooking for another 10 to 15 minutes, until top is fluffy and lightly browned. Spoon into serving bowls.

Warm Raspberry-Pear Cobbler

SERVES 6 TO 8

1	package (10 oz/300 g) frozen raspberries, thawed, drained, reserve liquid	1
1/3 cup	granulated sugar	75 mL
2 tsp	cornstarch	10 mL
1/2 tsp	ground cinnamon	2 mL
3 cups	peeled, sliced pears (about 3 medium)	750 mL
Topping		
1 cup	all-purpose flour	250 mL
1/2 cup	granulated sugar	125 mL
1 tsp	baking powder	5 mL
1/4 tsp	salt	1 mL
1	egg, lightly beaten	1
3/4 cup	sour cream	175 mL
2 tbsp	butter or margarine, melted	25 mL

TIP: Serve warm with whipped topping or ice cream.

- *Preheat oven to 350°F (180°C)*
- *13- by 9-inch (3 L) baking dish, ungreased*

1. Put reserved raspberry liquid into a measuring cup and add enough water to make it 1 cup (250 mL).
2. In a large saucepan, combine sugar, cornstarch, cinnamon and the 1 cup (250 mL) of syrup. Cook over medium heat until bubbly. Add the pears and raspberries and mix well until heated through. Spoon into baking dish and set aside.
3. *Prepare topping:* In a medium bowl, combine flour, sugar, baking powder and salt. Mix together. In a small bowl, whisk egg, sour cream and butter and stir into flour mixture. Mix until well blended. Drop by spoonfuls onto fruit mixture.
4. Bake in preheated oven for 25 to 30 minutes, or until topping is golden brown.

Pumpkin Cupcakes with Lemon Cream Cheese Frosting (page 21) ▶

Hawaiian Pineapple Cobbler

SERVES 6

⅓ cup	biscuit mix	75 mL
1 cup	granulated sugar	250 mL
1 tsp	grated lemon zest	5 mL
4 cups	fresh pineapple chunks (about 1 small pineapple)	1 L

Topping

¾ cup	biscuit mix	175 mL
⅔ cup	granulated sugar	150 mL
1	egg, lightly beaten	1
¼ cup	butter or margarine, melted	50 mL

- *Preheat oven to 350°F (180°C)*
- *9-inch (2.5 L) square baking pan or 9-inch (23 cm) pie plate, greased*

1. In a large bowl, mix together biscuit mix, sugar and zest. Add the pineapple chunks and mix to blend. Spoon into prepared baking pan.
2. *Prepare topping:* In a medium bowl, mix together biscuit mix, sugar and egg and sprinkle over fruit. Drizzle melted butter over top.
3. Bake in preheated oven for 40 to 45 minutes, or until topping is browned. Serve warm or at room temperature.

Fresh Plum Cobbler

SERVES 6

3 cups	sliced fresh plums (about 6 medium)	750 mL
¾ cup	pineapple chunks (fresh or canned)	175 mL
1 cup	granulated sugar	250 mL
¼ cup	cornstarch	50 mL
1 tbsp	butter or margarine	15 mL

Biscuit Topping

4 tsp	granulated sugar	20 mL
½ tsp	ground cinnamon	2 mL
1	roll (12 oz/340 g) refrigerated buttermilk biscuits	1
1 tbsp	butter or margarine, melted	15 mL

- *Preheat oven to 400°F (200°C)*
- *8-cup (2 L) shallow casserole dish, greased*

1. In a large bowl, combine plums, pineapple, sugar and cornstarch. Mix until well blended. Spoon into prepared casserole dish and dot with butter. Bake, uncovered, in preheated oven for 15 minutes.
2. *Prepare biscuit topping:* In a small bowl, mix together sugar and cinnamon. Separate biscuits and cut into quarters. Place biscuit pieces over hot plum mixture, brush melted butter over biscuits and sprinkle cinnamon-sugar mixture over top.
3. Return to oven and bake for another 25 to 30 minutes, or until top is golden brown.

Rhubarb Cobblecake

SERVES 4 TO 6

2 cups	washed, trimmed and diced rhubarb (about 10 oz/300 g)	500 mL
2/3 cup	liquid honey	150 mL
1 tbsp	all-purpose flour	15 mL
1 tsp	ground cinnamon	5 mL
1 tsp	grated orange zest	5 mL
Topping		
1 cup	all-purpose flour	250 mL
2 tsp	baking powder	10 mL
1/2 tsp	salt	2 mL
1/4 cup	butter or shortening	50 mL
1	egg, lightly beaten	1
3 tbsp	milk	45 mL
2 tbsp	liquid honey	25 mL

- *Preheat oven to 350°F (180°C)*
- *8-inch (2 L) square baking pan, well greased*

1. In a large bowl, mix together rhubarb, honey, flour, cinnamon and zest. Pour into prepared baking pan.
2. *Prepare topping:* In another large bowl, combine flour, baking powder and salt. Cut in butter with a pastry blender or two knives until mixture is crumbly.
3. In a small bowl, mix together egg, milk and honey. Pour into flour mixture and stir only until mixture is moistened and blended, or until you have a stiff batter. Drop batter by spoonfuls onto rhubarb mixture.
4. Bake in preheated oven for 30 to 35 minutes, or until topping is golden brown. Serve warm.

Strawberry-Rhubarb Cobbler

SERVES ABOUT 9

1	package (20 oz/600 g) sliced frozen rhubarb, thawed	1
1	package (10 oz/300 g) frozen strawberries, thawed	1
1/2 to 3/4 cups	granulated sugar	125 to 175 mL
Topping		
2 cups	all-purpose flour	500 mL
2 tbsp	granulated sugar	25 mL
1 tbsp	baking powder	15 mL
1 tsp	salt	5 mL
2/3 cup	milk	150 mL
1/3 cup	vegetable oil	75 mL
	Butter or margarine	
1 tsp	ground cinnamon	5 mL
2 tbsp	granulated sugar	25 mL

- *Preheat oven to 450°F (230°C)*
- *9-inch (2.5 L) square baking dish, ungreased*

1. In a large bowl, combine rhubarb, strawberries and sugar, mixing well. Pour into baking dish.
2. *Prepare topping:* In another large bowl, mix together flour, sugar, baking powder and salt. Make a well in the center. Add milk and oil and stir until mixture forms a ball of dough. Divide dough into 9 biscuits and place biscuits atop the fruit in the baking dish. Make an indentation in each biscuit and dot with butter.
3. In a small bowl, mix together sugar and cinnamon. Sprinkle the cinnamon-sugar mixture over top.
4. Bake at 450°F (230°C) for 25 minutes, or until topping is golden brown. Serve warm or at room temperature.

Crumbles

Apple Crumble

SERVES 6

1 tsp	ground cinnamon	5 mL
7	large apples, peeled and thinly sliced	7

Topping

¾ cup	all-purpose flour	175 mL
¾ cup	old-fashioned rolled oats	175 mL
½ cup	granulated sugar	125 mL
½ cup	butter or margarine	125 mL

TIP: Serve warm, with Quick Custard Sauce (see page 176), ice cream or whipped cream.

VARIATION: You could use ¼ cup (50 mL) oat bran and ½ cup (125 mL) of quick-cooking oats instead of the ¾ cup (175 mL) of rolled oats.

- *Preheat oven to 350°F (180°C)*
- *6-cup (1.5 L) casserole dish, greased*

1. In a large bowl, mix together ¼ cup (50 mL) water and cinnamon. Add apples and toss together until well mixed. Pour into prepared casserole dish.
2. *Prepare topping:* In a medium bowl, combine flour, oats and sugar. Cut in butter or margarine with a pastry blender or two knives until mixture resembles coarse crumbs. Spoon over apple mixture.
3. Bake in preheated oven for 45 to 50 minutes, or until topping is golden brown.

Apple-Pear Crumble

SERVES 4 TO 6

½ cup	old-fashioned rolled oats	125 mL
⅓ cup	all-purpose flour, sifted	75 mL
¼ cup	ground almonds	50 mL
2 tbsp	butter or margarine	25 mL
3	medium apples, cored and chopped (I use Granny Smith)	3
2	medium pears, cored and chopped	2
¼ cup	raisins (optional)	50 mL
2 tsp	lemon zest (optional)	10 mL
3 tbsp	freshly squeezed lemon juice	45 mL
½ cup	packed brown sugar	125 mL
½ tsp	ground allspice	2 mL

- *Preheat oven to 350°F (180°C)*
- *6-cup (1.5 L) casserole dish, greased*

1. In a small bowl, mix together oats, flour and almonds. Cut in butter, using your hands or a pastry blender. Set aside.
2. Place apples, pears, raisins (if using), lemon zest (if using) and lemon juice into prepared casserole dish.
3. In another small bowl, mix together brown sugar and allspice. Sprinkle over fruit in baking dish. Then sprinkle oat mixture over top.
4. Bake in preheated oven for 25 to 30 minutes, or until fruit is tender and top is golden brown. Serve warm.

Canned Apple Crunch

SERVES 6

1	package (12 oz/350 g) shortbread cookies, finely crushed	1
½ cup	firmly packed brown sugar, divided	125 mL
1	can (19 oz/540 mL) pie-sliced apples, well-drained	1
2 tbsp	butter or margarine	25 mL
¼ cup	granulated sugar	50 mL
1 tsp	ground cinnamon	5 mL

TIP: Serve warm, with Quick Custard Sauce (see page 176).

- *Preheat oven to 350°F (180°C)*
- *8-inch (2 L) square baking pan, greased*

1. In a medium bowl, combine cookie crumbs and ¼ cup (50 mL) of the brown sugar. Mix well. Press about one-third of the crumb mixture into prepared baking pan.

2. Place apples in a blender and process until smooth. Pour into another medium bowl and add the remaining ¼ cup (50 mL) of brown sugar.

3. In a small bowl, mix together sugar and cinnamon.

4. Spoon about half of the apple mixture over the crumb mixture in pan. Spoon in another third of the crumb mixture. Spoon in remaining apple mixture and then top with the remaining crumb mixture. Dot with butter and sprinkle sugar-cinnamon mixture lightly over top.

5. Bake in preheated oven for 25 to 30 minutes, or until firm and golden brown.

Cran-Apple Almond Crumble

SERVES 8 TO 10

1 cup	granulated sugar, divided	250 mL
4 tsp	grated orange zest	20 mL
1 cup	freshly squeezed orange juice	250 mL
1½ cups	fresh or frozen, thawed cranberries (about 6 oz/175 g)	375 mL
2 tbsp	butter or margarine	25 mL
2 tbsp	liquid honey	25 mL
2 tbsp	maple syrup	25 mL
5	Granny Smith apples, peeled and cut into ½-inch (1 cm) slices	5
2 tbsp	quick-cooking tapioca	25 mL

Topping

1½ cups	all-purpose flour	375 mL
¾ cup	firmly packed brown sugar	175 mL
2 tsp	ground cinnamon	10 mL
½ tsp	ground nutmeg	2 mL
½ cup	cold butter or margarine	125 mL
3 tbsp	almond paste	45 mL
1 cup	slivered almonds, toasted (optional)	250 mL

- *Preheat oven to 400°F (200°C)*
- *13- by 9-inch (3 L) baking dish, greased*

1. In a medium saucepan, over medium heat, combine ¾ cup (175 mL) of the sugar, orange zest and juice and bring to a boil. Lower heat to simmer and cook uncovered, stirring, for about 5 to 6 minutes. Add cranberries and continue to simmer for 10 minutes, or until the berries begin popping. Remove from heat.

2. In a large saucepan, melt the butter and add honey, syrup and the remaining ¼ cup (50 mL) sugar. Pour in apples and cook over medium heat for about 5 minutes. Remove from heat and pour into the cranberry mixture. Sprinkle tapioca over top and mix until well blended. Set aside for 15 minutes. Spoon into prepared baking dish.

3. *Prepare topping:* In a medium bowl, combine flour, brown sugar, cinnamon and nutmeg. Cut in butter and almond paste until mixture resembles coarse crumbs.

4. Sprinkle topping over cranberry mixture and sprinkle almonds over top, if desired. Bake in preheated oven for 20 minutes, or until bubbly and golden brown.

Turnover Cranberry Crumble

SERVES 6

3 cups	fresh or frozen, thawed cranberries (about 12 oz/375 g)	750 mL
1¾ cup	granulated sugar, divided	425 mL
½ cup	chopped nuts (pecans or other)	125 mL
2	eggs	2
1 cup	all-purpose flour	250 mL
½ cup	butter or margarine, melted	125 mL

- *Preheat oven to 325°F (160°C)*
- *8-inch (2 L) square baking dish, greased*

1. Spoon cranberries into prepared baking dish and sprinkle with ¾ cup (175 mL) of the sugar and chopped nuts. Toss together until well blended.

2. In a large mixer bowl, combine eggs, flour, melted butter and the remaining 1 cup (250 mL) of sugar and beat until blended and smooth. Spread evenly over cranberry mixture.

3. Bake in preheated oven for 55 to 60 minutes, or until golden brown. Run a knife around the edges of the dish and invert immediately onto a serving platter. Serve warm.

Peach Crumble

SERVES 6

1 cup	all-purpose flour	250 mL
¾ cup	packed brown sugar, divided	175 mL
¼ tsp	salt	1 mL
¼ cup	butter or margarine	50 mL
6	medium peaches, peeled, pitted and thinly sliced	6
¼ tsp	ground mace	1 mL

TIP: Serve warm with whipped topping.

- *Preheat oven to 350°F (180°C)*
- *6-cup (1.5 L) casserole dish, buttered*

1. In a medium bowl, combine flour, ½ cup (125 mL) of the brown sugar and salt and mix well. Cut in butter with your hands or a pastry blender until mixture is crumbly. Set aside.

2. In a large bowl, combine peach slices, the remaining ¼ cup (50 mL) brown sugar and mace and toss to blend. Spoon into prepared casserole dish.

3. Spread crumbly mixture over the peaches and pat down lightly.

4. Bake in preheated oven for 40 to 45 minutes, or until golden brown.

Pineapple Coconut Crumble

SERVES 6

1 cup	sweetened flaked coconut	250 mL
2	cans (each 19 oz/540 mL) pineapple chunks, drained, juice reserved (or use 5 cups/ 1.25 L fresh pineapple)	2
¼ cup	reserved pineapple juice	50 mL
1 cup	all-purpose flour	250 mL
⅔ cup	firmly packed brown sugar	150 mL
¼ tsp	baking powder	1 mL
½ cup	butter or margarine, melted and cooled	125 mL
1 cup	coarsely chopped macadamia (or other) nuts	250 mL

- *Preheat oven to 350°F (180°C)*
- *8-cup (2 L) casserole dish, ungreased*
- *Rimmed baking sheet*

1. Spread coconut on baking sheet and bake in preheated oven for 10 minutes, or until lightly browned. Set aside to cool. Keep the oven heated to 350°F (180°C).
2. Spoon pineapple chunks and the reserved liquid into casserole dish. Cover tightly and bake for 15 to 20 minutes, or until hot.
3. In a medium bowl, combine flour, brown sugar and baking powder and mix well. Add the butter and mix with your fingers until evenly moistened. Add the coconut and nuts and stir to form a large clump. Break into small pieces and scatter evenly over the hot pineapple.
4. Bake for 30 to 35 minutes, or until golden brown and bubbly and fruit is tender. Serve warm or at room temperature.

Raspberry and Pear Crumble

SERVES 6

4 cups	peeled and sliced pears (about 4 medium)	1 L
2 cups	frozen raspberries (about 12 oz/375 g)	500 mL
⅓ cup	lightly packed brown sugar	75 mL
2 tbsp	all-purpose flour	25 mL
½ tsp	ground nutmeg	2 mL
Topping		
¾ cup	all-purpose flour	175 mL
¾ cup	quick-cooking rolled oats	175 mL
¾ cup	lightly packed brown sugar	175 mL
⅓ cup	butter or margarine, melted	75 mL

- *Preheat oven to 350°F (180°C)*
- *8-inch (2 L) square baking dish, ungreased*

1. In a large bowl, combine pears, raspberries, brown sugar, flour and nutmeg and toss together gently to blend. Spoon into baking dish.
2. *Prepare topping:* In another large bowl, combine flour, oats and brown sugar and mix well. Drizzle in the melted butter and mix together until mixture is crumbly. Sprinkle topping over fruit mixture.
3. Bake in preheated oven for 45 to 50 minutes, or until bubbly, golden brown and fruit is tender.

Tropical Fruit Crunch

SERVES 6

2 cups	fresh fruit, such as 1 ripe pineapple, 2 small mangos and 1 large ripe banana, or any other suitable fruits, such as papaya, melons, etc., each peeled, cored and cut into 1-inch (2.5 cm) chunks	500 mL
	Juice of ½ lime	
½ to ¾ cup	granulated sugar	125 to 175 mL
2 tbsp	quick-cooking tapioca	25 mL

Topping

1 cup	sifted all-purpose flour	250 mL
½ cup	granulated sugar	125 mL
½ cup	packed brown sugar	125 mL
⅔ cup	cold butter or margarine, cut into small chunks	150 mL
⅓ cup	sweetened shredded coconut	75 mL
½ cup	chopped nuts (optional)	125 mL

TIP: Serve warm, or at room temperature, with a dollop of yogurt, ice cream or a sauce, topped with a chunk of fruit.

- *Preheat oven to 375°F (190°C)*
- *8-cup (2 L) casserole dish, ungreased*

1. In a large bowl, combine the prepared fruit. Sprinkle with lime juice and toss gently to coat.

2. In a small bowl, mix together sugar and tapioca. Toss in with the fruit. Spoon fruit into casserole dish.

3. *Prepare topping:* In a large bowl, mix together flour, sugar and brown sugar. Cut in butter with a pastry blender or two knives until mixture resembles coarse crumbs. Stir in coconut and nuts, if using, and sprinkle evenly over fruit.

4. Bake in preheated oven for 40 to 45 minutes, or until bubbly and topping is golden brown.

Apple-Rhubarb Oat Crumble

SERVES 6

1½ cups	apples, peeled and diced (about 1½ medium)	375 mL
1 cup	frozen rhubarb, diced	250 mL
½ cup	lightly packed brown sugar	125 mL
2 tbsp	all-purpose flour	25 mL
1 tsp	ground cinnamon	5 mL
½ tsp	ground nutmeg	2 mL
¼ tsp	salt	1 mL
1 cup	sour cream	250 mL

Topping

1½ cups	quick-cooking rolled oats	375 mL
½ cup	granulated sugar	125 mL
½ cup	chopped nuts (optional)	125 mL
2 tbsp	all-purpose flour	25 mL
¾ cup	butter or margarine, melted	175 mL

- *Preheat oven to 350°F (180°C)*
- *8- or 9-inch (2 or 2.5 L) square baking pan, ungreased*

1. In a large bowl, combine apples and rhubarb. Add brown sugar, flour, cinnamon, nutmeg and salt and mix together to blend. Add sour cream and mix until well blended. Spoon into baking pan.

2. *Prepare topping:* In another large bowl, combine oats, sugar, nuts (if using) and flour. Stir in melted butter and mix until mixture resembles coarse crumbs. Sprinkle over apple-rhubarb mixture.

3. Bake in preheated oven for 25 to 30 minutes, or until apples are fork-tender and top is golden brown.

Crisps

Scrumptious Apple Crisp

SERVES 8 TO 10

6 to 8	medium apples, peeled, cored and cut into slices	6 to 8
	Ground cinnamon	
	Granulated sugar	

Topping

1 1/2 cups	lightly packed brown sugar	375 mL
1 cup	all-purpose flour	250 mL
1 tsp	baking powder	5 mL
1/4 tsp	salt	1 mL
1	egg	1
1/4 cup	butter or margarine, melted	50 mL

TIP: Best when served warm with ice cream or any other topping.

VARIATION: Use 2 cans (each 19 oz/540 mL) of apple pie filling mixed with 1 tsp (5 mL) freshly squeezed lemon juice and 1 tsp (5 mL) ground cinnamon. Then add the topping and bake as above.

- *Preheat oven to 375°F (190°C)*
- *13- by 9-inch (3 L) baking dish or 9-inch (2.5 L) square baking dish, ungreased*

1. Layer apple slices in baking dish. After each layer, sprinkle some cinnamon and sugar (according to taste) over top before adding another layer.
2. *Prepare topping:* In a medium bowl, mix together brown sugar, flour, baking powder, salt and egg. Mix well until blended. Sprinkle over the apples, then drizzle the melted butter over top.
3. Bake in preheated oven for 35 to 40 minutes, or until topping is golden brown and crisp.

Mom's Old-Fashioned Apple Crisp

SERVES 4 TO 6

4 cups	peeled, cored and sliced tart apples (about 4 medium)	1 L
3/4 cup	firmly packed brown sugar	175 mL
1/2 cup	quick-cooking rolled oats	125 mL
1/2 cup	all-purpose flour	125 mL
1 1/2 tsp	ground cinnamon	7 mL
1/4 tsp	ground allspice (optional)	1 mL
Pinch	ground nutmeg	Pinch
1/3 cup	cold butter or margarine	75 mL

TIP: Serve warm with whipped topping or ice cream.

- *Preheat oven to 375°F (190°C)*
- *8- or 9-inch (2 or 2.5 L) square baking dish, greased*

1. Place apple slices into prepared baking dish.
2. In a medium bowl, combine brown sugar, oats, flour, cinnamon, allspice and nutmeg. Cut in butter with a pastry blender or two knives until mixture resembles coarse crumbs. Spoon evenly over apples.
3. Bake in preheated oven for 30 to 35 minutes, or until apples are tender and topping is golden brown.

Microwave Apple Graham Crisp

SERVES 6

6 to 8	medium tart apples, peeled, cored and sliced	6 to 8
1 cup	graham cracker crumbs (about 12 wafers)	250 mL
½ cup	packed brown sugar	125 mL
½ cup	all-purpose flour	125 mL
1½ tsp	ground cinnamon	7 mL
½ tsp	ground nutmeg	2 mL
½ cup	butter or margarine, melted	125 mL

- *8-cup (2 L) microwave-safe casserole dish, greased*

1. Place apple slices into prepared casserole dish.

2. In a medium bowl, combine graham cracker crumbs, brown sugar, flour, cinnamon and nutmeg and mix together until well incorporated. Stir in melted butter and mix well. Sprinkle over apple slices.

3. Microwave, uncovered, on High for 12 minutes, or until apples become tender. Best when served warm.

Very Berry Apple Crisp

SERVES 6 TO 8

6	Granny Smith apples, peeled, cored and cut into bite-size chunks	6
2 cups	berries (your choice of blueberries, strawberries, cranberries, raspberries or others), fresh or frozen	500 mL
¾ cup	granulated sugar (more or less, depending on tartness of apples)	175 mL
2 tbsp	all-purpose flour	25 mL
1 to 2 tsp	ground cinnamon	5 to 10 mL
½ tsp	ground nutmeg	2 mL
Topping		
¾ cup	old-fashioned rolled oats	175 mL
2 tbsp	lightly packed brown sugar	25 mL
2 tbsp	all-purpose flour	25 mL
3 tbsp	butter or margarine, softened	45 mL

- *Preheat oven to 375°F (190°C)*
- *8- or 9-inch (2 or 2.5 L) square baking dish, ungreased*

1. In a large bowl, combine apples, berries, sugar, flour, cinnamon and nutmeg. Toss together until well incorporated. Spoon into baking dish.

2. *Prepare topping:* In a small bowl, combine oats, brown sugar and flour. Add butter and stir until moist and crumbly. Sprinkle topping over apple mixture.

3. Bake in preheated oven for 50 to 60 minutes, or until filling is bubbly and topping is golden brown. Serve warm or at room temperature.

TIP: Use one type of berries or combine them as you please.

Cheesy Apple Crisp

SERVES 6

6 to 8	Granny Smith apples, peeled, cored and sliced	6 to 8
¾ cup	granulated sugar (more or less, depending on tartness of apples)	175 mL
⅔ cup	all-purpose flour	150 mL
½ cup	butter or margarine	125 mL
½ cup	shredded Cheddar cheese (sharp or according to taste, about 2 oz/60 g)	125 mL
1½ tsp	ground cinnamon	7 mL

- *Preheat oven to 375°F (190°C)*
- *6-cup (1.5 L) casserole dish, buttered*

1. Place apple slices into prepared casserole dish. Pour ½ cup (125 mL) water over the apple slices.
2. In a large bowl, combine sugar and flour. Cut in butter with a pastry blender or two knives until mixture resembles coarse crumbs. Stir in cheese and cinnamon, mixing together well. Sprinkle over apple slices.
3. Bake in preheated oven for 40 to 45 minutes, or until apples are tender and top is golden brown.

Fruit Jam Apple Betty

SERVES 6

2 cups	peeled, cored and chopped apples (about 2 medium)	500 mL
½ cup	fruit jam or marmalade (orange, pineapple, rhubarb or other)	125 mL
3 cups	fresh bread crumbs (about 6 slices)	750 mL
2 tbsp	butter or margarine, softened	25 mL
	Light brown sugar	
	Ground nutmeg	

- *Preheat oven to 350°F (180°C)*
- *9-inch (2.5 L) square baking dish, buttered*

1. In a medium bowl, mix together apples and jam. Set aside.
2. In a large bowl, mix together bread crumbs and butter until crumbly. Sprinkle a layer of crumbs into prepared baking dish. Top with some of the apple-jam mixture. Sprinkle a little nutmeg and brown sugar over top. Repeat with another layer of each.
3. Bake in preheated oven for 35 to 45 minutes, or until golden brown.

TIP: To make fresh bread crumbs, process bread slices in a food processor or blender until crumbs are the desired size. Store in an airtight container in the refrigerator for up to 1 week or in the freezer for up to 6 months.

Bumbleberry Crisp

SERVES 8

1½ cups	peeled, cored and chopped tart apples (about 1½ medium)	375 mL
1½ cups	finely chopped rhubarb, fresh or frozen (about 10 oz/300 g)	375 mL
1½ cups	fresh or frozen blueberries (about 10 oz/300 g)	375 mL
1½ cups	fresh or frozen raspberries (about 10 oz/300 g)	375 mL
¾ cup	granulated sugar	175 mL
¼ cup	quick-cooking tapioca	50 mL
1½ tsp	ground cinnamon	7 mL

Topping

½ cup	firmly packed brown sugar	125 mL
½ cup	all-purpose flour	125 mL
⅓ cup	butter or margarine	75 mL
½ cup	old-fashioned rolled oats	125 mL
¼ cup	sliced almonds (optional)	50 mL

- *Preheat oven to 350°F (180°C)*
- *13- by 9-inch (3 L) baking dish, buttered*

1. In a large bowl, combine apples, rhubarb, blueberries and raspberries. Add sugar, tapioca and cinnamon and toss together until well blended. Spoon into prepared baking dish.

2. *Prepare topping:* In a medium bowl, combine brown sugar and flour. Cut in butter by hand, using your fingertips so that mixture is crumbly. Mix in rolled oats and almonds, if using. Sprinkle topping over fruit mixture, spreading evenly.

3. Bake in preheated oven for 40 to 45 minutes, or until topping is golden brown and fruit is bubbly. Serve warm.

Lemon Coconut Crisp

SERVES 6

Crust

¾ cup	packed brown sugar	175 mL
⅓ cup + 1 tbsp	butter or margarine, softened	90 mL
18	saltine crackers, finely crushed	18
1 cup	all-purpose flour	250 mL
½ cup	flaked coconut	125 mL
½ tsp	salt	2 mL
½ tsp	baking soda	2 mL

Filling

¾ cup	granulated sugar	175 mL
2 tbsp	cornstarch	25 mL
¼ tsp	salt	1 mL
2	egg yolks, lightly beaten	2
½ tsp	grated lemon zest	2 mL
½ cup	freshly squeezed lemon juice	125 mL

TIP: Serve warm with whipped topping or a sauce.

- *Preheat oven to 350°F (180°C)*
- *8-inch (2 L) square baking pan, ungreased*

1. *Prepare crust:* In a large bowl, cream brown sugar and butter until smooth. Add crushed crackers, flour, coconut, salt and baking soda and stir until well mixed. Press half of this mixture into baking pan and bake in preheated oven for 10 minutes. Set aside to cool. Keep the oven heated to 350°F (180°C).

2. *Prepare filling:* In a medium saucepan, over low heat, combine sugar, cornstarch and salt. Gradually stir in 1 cup (250 mL) hot water. Cook, stirring constantly, until mixture is boiling and thick; boil for about 2 to 3 minutes. Remove from heat.

3. In a small bowl, beat egg yolks lightly. Add a small amount of the hot cornstarch mixture into the egg yolks and return this egg mixture back to saucepan. Bring to a boil, stirring constantly, then remove from heat. Stir in the lemon zest and juice and spoon over baked crumb crust. Top with the remaining crumb mixture.

4. Bake for 30 to 35 minutes, or until top is golden brown.

Springtime Fruit Crisp

SERVES 8 TO 12

4	medium apples, peeled, cored and thinly sliced	4
2 lbs	fresh rhubarb, chopped (about 7 cups/1.75 L)	1 kg
4	ripe medium mangoes, pitted, chopped and peeled into ½-inch (1 cm) chunks	4
1	small pineapple, peeled, cut into quarters, cored and chopped into bite-size chunks	1
1 cup	golden raisins	250 mL
½ cup	chopped nuts (pecans, or other)	125 mL
1½ cups	all-purpose flour, divided	375 mL
1½ cups	packed brown sugar, divided	375 mL
2 tsp	ground cinnamon, divided	10 mL
¾ cup	butter or margarine, softened	175 mL

- *Preheat oven to 350°F (180°C)*
- *13- by 9-inch (3 L) baking dish, buttered*

1. In a large bowl, combine apples, rhubarb, mango and pineapple and mix well. Add raisins and nuts and toss together until well blended.

2. In a small bowl, mix together ½ cup (125 mL) of the brown sugar, ¼ cup (50 mL) of the flour and 1 tsp (5 mL) of cinnamon. Sprinkle over bowl of fruit and toss and mix until well incorporated and blended.

3. Pour fruit mixture into prepared baking dish, pressing fruit down with your hands to pack mixture down tightly.

4. Combine remaining 1¼ cups (300 mL) flour, 1 cup (250 mL) brown sugar and 1 tsp (5 mL) cinnamon. Cut in butter with your fingertips, a fork or a pastry blender until mixture resembles coarse crumbs. Sprinkle over mixture in baking dish.

5. Bake in preheated oven for 1 to 1½ hours, or until golden brown and fruit is tender and bubbly. Allow to stand for about 10 minutes before serving.

Favorite Peach Crisp

SERVES 6 TO 8

Crust

1 cup	all-purpose flour	250 mL
½ cup	firmly packed brown sugar	125 mL
Pinch	salt	Pinch
½ cup	butter or margarine, softened	125 mL

Filling

¾ cup	granulated sugar	175 mL
¼ cup	cornstarch	50 mL
2	cans (each 14 oz/398 mL) sliced peaches, drained, reserving juice	2

Topping

1 ½ cups	old-fashioned rolled oats	375 mL
½ cup	firmly packed brown sugar	125 mL
¼ cup	all-purpose flour	50 mL
⅓ cup	butter or margarine, softened	75 mL

- *Preheat oven to 350°F (180°C)*
- *9-inch (2.5 L) square baking dish, greased*

1. *Prepare crust:* In a medium bowl, combine flour, brown sugar and salt. Cut in butter by hand, using your fingertips or a fork, until mixture resembles coarse crumbs. Pat down into prepared baking dish and bake in preheated oven for 15 minutes. Keep the oven heated to 350°F (180°C).

2. *Prepare filling:* In a medium saucepan, bring sugar, cornstarch and reserved juice to a boil, stirring constantly, and boil for 2 minutes, or until thickened. Remove from heat and stir in peach slices. Spoon into baked crust.

3. *Prepare topping:* In a large bowl, combine oats, brown sugar and flour. Cut in butter with a fork or pastry blender until mixture resembles coarse crumbs. Sprinkle over filling.

4. Bake for 25 to 30 minutes, or until topping is golden brown and fruit is bubbly.

Traditional Raspberry Crisp

SERVES 6 TO 8

4 cups	fresh or frozen raspberries (about 1 ½ lbs/750 g)	1 L
3 tbsp + ⅓ cup	all-purpose flour,	45 mL + 75 mL
⅓ cup	granulated sugar	75 mL
¾ cup	quick-cooking rolled oats	175 mL
⅓ cup	firmly packed brown sugar	75 mL
¼ cup	cold butter or margarine	50 mL

- *Preheat oven to 350°F (180°C)*
- *9-inch (2.5 L) square baking dish, greased*

1. In a medium bowl, toss together raspberries, the 3 tbsp (45 mL) flour and granulated sugar. Spoon into prepared baking dish.

2. In a large bowl, combine oats, brown sugar and the ⅓ cup (75 mL) flour. Cut in butter, using a fork, your fingertips or a pastry blender, until mixture is crumbly. Sprinkle over fruit mixture.

3. Bake in preheated oven for 25 to 30 minutes, or until top is golden brown.

Spiced Pear Crisp

SERVES 8

8 to 10	ripe pears, peeled, cored and sliced	8 to 10
2 tbsp	freshly squeezed lemon juice	25 mL
¾ cup	packed brown sugar, divided	175 mL
2 tsp	ground ginger	10 mL
¼ tsp	ground nutmeg	1 mL
¼ tsp	ground cloves	1 mL
1 cup	all-purpose flour	250 mL
½ cup	whole wheat flour	125 mL
½ tsp	salt	2 mL
½ cup	butter or margarine, cut into pieces	125 mL

- *Preheat oven to 350°F (180°C)*
- *9-inch (2.5 L) square baking dish, ungreased*

1. Place pear slices in a large bowl and toss with the lemon juice. Add ¼ cup (50 mL) of the brown sugar, ginger, nutmeg and cloves and stir until well blended. Spoon into baking dish.

2. In another large bowl, mix together flours, salt and the remaining ½ cup (125 mL) brown sugar. Cut in butter with a pastry blender or two knives until mixture resembles coarse crumbs. Sprinkle over pear mixture, spreading evenly.

3. Bake in preheated oven for 45 to 50 minutes, or until topping is golden brown and filling is bubbly. Serve warm.

Plum Good Apricot Crisp

SERVES 8 TO 10

1½ lbs	fresh plums, pitted and quartered	750 g
1 lb	fresh apricots, pitted and quartered	500 g
½ cup	granulated sugar (or to taste)	125 mL
3 tbsp	all-purpose flour	45 mL
Topping		
¾ cup	all-purpose flour	175 mL
⅓ cup	light brown sugar, packed	75 mL
¼ cup	old-fashioned rolled oats	50 mL
¼ cup	chopped nuts	50 mL
1 tbsp	granulated sugar	15 mL
½ tsp	ground cinnamon	2 mL
¼ cup	butter or margarine	50 mL

- *Preheat oven to 400°F (200°C)*
- *13- by 9-inch (3 L) baking dish, ungreased*

1. Spoon plums and apricots into baking dish. Sprinkle sugar and flour over fruit.

2. *Prepare topping:* In a large bowl, combine flour, brown sugar, oats, nuts, sugar and cinnamon. Cut in butter with a pastry blender or two knives until mixture resembles coarse crumbs (or process in food processor). Spread topping over the fruit, spreading evenly.

3. Bake in preheated oven for 35 to 40 minutes, or until topping is golden brown and fruit is tender and bubbly. Serve warm.

Zucchini Oat Crisp

SERVES 6 TO 8

2	medium zucchini, peeled and cut into slices	2
2 cups	all-purpose flour	500 mL
1 cup	quick-cooking rolled oats	250 mL
3/4 cup	packed brown sugar	175 mL
2/3 cup	butter or margarine, softened	150 mL
1/3 cup	freshly squeezed lemon juice	75 mL
1/3 cup	granulated sugar	75 mL
1 1/2 tsp	ground cinnamon	7 mL

- *Preheat oven to 375°F (190°C)*
- *9-inch (2.5 L) square baking dish, greased*

1. Put zucchini slices in a medium saucepan and add enough water just to cover. Cook over medium heat until tender. Drain and set aside.

2. In a large bowl, combine flour, oats and brown sugar. Cut in butter with a pastry blender until mixture resembles coarse crumbs. Pat half of this crumb mixture into bottom of prepared baking dish and bake in preheated oven for 10 minutes. Remove from oven.

3. Place cooked zucchini slices on baked crust. Sprinkle lemon juice, sugar and cinnamon over filling. Top with remaining crumb mixture.

4. Bake for another 30 to 35 minutes, or until topping is golden brown. Serve warm.

Colleen's Rhubarb Crisp

SERVES 6 TO 8

2 lbs	raw rhubarb, cut into 1/2-inch (1 cm) pieces (about 7 cups/1.75 L)	1 kg
1	egg, lightly beaten	1
3/4 cup	granulated sugar	175 mL
2 tbsp	all-purpose flour	25 mL
1/2 tsp	ground cinnamon	2 mL
Topping		
3/4 cup	old-fashioned rolled oats	175 mL
1/3 cup	packed brown sugar	75 mL
1/4 cup	all-purpose flour	50 mL
1 tsp	ground cinnamon	5 mL
1/4 cup	cold butter or margarine	50 mL

TIP: Serve warm with whipped topping or ice cream.

- *Preheat oven to 375°F (190°C)*
- *9-inch (2.5 L) square glass baking dish, buttered*

1. In a large bowl, toss together rhubarb, egg, sugar, flour and cinnamon until well incorporated and blended. Pour into prepared baking dish.

2. *Prepare topping:* In a small bowl, combine oats, brown sugar, flour and cinnamon. Cut in butter with a fork or pastry blender until mixture resembles coarse crumbs. Sprinkle over rhubarb mixture.

3. Bake in preheated oven for 40 minutes, or until topping is golden brown.

Strawberry-Rhubarb Crisp

SERVES 6

2 lbs	fresh rhubarb, cut into ½-inch (1 cm) pieces (about 7 cups/1.75 L)	1 kg
1½ lbs	fresh strawberries, hulled and sliced in half lengthwise	750 g
	Grated zest of 1 orange	
	Juice of ½ orange	
⅔ cup	granulated sugar	150 mL
3 tbsp	all-purpose flour	45 mL
Topping		
1 cup	old-fashioned rolled oats	250 mL
¾ cup	all-purpose flour	175 mL
¾ cup	firmly packed brown sugar	175 mL
1 tsp	ground cinnamon	5 mL
Pinch	ground nutmeg	Pinch
½ cup	cold butter or margarine, cut into cubes	125 mL

- *Preheat oven to 350°F (180°C)*
- *12-cup (3 L) casserole dish, ungreased*

1. In a large bowl, combine rhubarb, strawberries, orange zest and juice. Toss together until well blended.
2. In a small bowl, mix together sugar and flour. Stir into the fruit mixture, mixing until well incorporated. Spoon into casserole dish.
3. *Prepare topping:* In a medium bowl, combine oats, flour, brown sugar, cinnamon and nutmeg. Cut in butter cubes with your fingertips or a pastry blender until mixture resembles coarse crumbs. Sprinkle topping over fruit, spreading evenly.
4. Bake in preheated oven for 30 to 35 minutes, or until fruit filling is bubbly and topping is golden brown. Cool before serving.

Quick Apple Brown Betty

SERVES 6 TO 8

2½ cups	canned apple pie filling	625 mL
1	package (18 oz/510 g) spice cake mix	1
⅓ cup + 1 tbsp	butter or margarine, melted	90 mL

- *Preheat oven to 350°F (180°C)*
- *9-inch (2.5 L) square baking dish, buttered*

1. Spoon pie filling into prepared baking dish. Sprinkle the cake mix evenly over apple filling. Then drizzle the melted butter over top.
2. Bake in preheated oven for 45 minutes, or until topping is golden brown. Serve either warm or cold.

Cran-Apple Pecan Crisp

SERVES 6

3 cups	peeled, cored and chopped Granny Smith apples (about 3 medium)	750 mL
2 cups	fresh or frozen, thawed cranberries (about 8 oz/250 g)	500 mL
1 cup	granulated sugar	250 mL
3 tbsp	all-purpose flour	45 mL
Topping		
1 ½ cups	quick-cooking rolled oats	375 mL
½ cup	all-purpose flour	125 mL
½ cup	firmly packed brown sugar	125 mL
½ cup	butter or margarine, melted	125 mL
⅓ cup	chopped pecans	75 mL

- *Preheat oven to 350°F (180°C)*
- *9-inch (2.5 L) square baking dish, greased*

1. In a large bowl, toss together apples, cranberries, sugar and flour. Spoon into prepared baking dish.
2. *Prepare topping:* In the same large bowl, combine oats, flour and brown sugar. Mix well and stir in melted butter and then pecans until well blended and crumbly. Sprinkle topping over apples.
3. Bake in preheated oven for 50 to 60 minutes, or until topping is golden brown and the fruit is tender. Serve warm.

Apple Nut Crisp

SERVES 6 TO 8

6 to 8	medium tart apples, peeled, cored and sliced	6 to 8
¼ cup	packed brown sugar	50 mL
2 tsp	ground cinnamon	10 mL
Topping		
2 cups	firmly packed brown sugar	500 mL
1 cup	butter or margarine, softened	250 mL
2	eggs	2
2 cups	all-purpose flour	500 mL
1 cup	finely chopped walnuts, divided	250 mL

- *Preheat oven to 350°F (180°C)*
- *13- by 9-inch (3 L) baking dish, greased*

1. Place apple slices into prepared baking dish. Sprinkle the brown sugar and cinnamon over top.
2. *Prepare topping:* In a large mixer bowl, cream brown sugar and butter. Add eggs, beating after each egg. Stir in the flour and ½ cup (125 mL) of the walnuts. Spread mixture over apples. Sprinkle the remaining walnuts over top.
3. Bake in preheated oven for 45 to 50 minutes, or until topping is golden brown and apples are tender. Serve warm.

Popovers

To make scrumptious popovers, use a heavy cast-iron popover pan. If you do not have a special pan, use a metal muffin pan or individual glass custard cups. The pans or cups should be filled about half-full. If you use custard cups, they should be placed on a baking sheet for easier handling. Spray the cups with nonstick cooking spray.

Popover batter can be prepared in a bowl by whisking the ingredients together until blended and smooth and the consistency of the batter is similar to heavy cream. Be careful not to over-beat or the popovers may not rise as high as they should. If you are not planning to make the popovers immediately, store batter in a covered container in the refrigerator for 3 to 4 hours or overnight. Stir before using.

Do not open the oven door to peek during baking, and do not under-bake, as this could cause the popovers to collapse. Be patient, and you will be rewarded with puffy, delicious popovers.

Baked popovers are moist inside from the steam that makes them rise and be puffy, so about 5 minutes before popovers are done, remove them from the oven and quickly prick each in two or three places with a fork or a pointed knife to let the steam escape. Turn the oven off and return popovers to the oven for the remaining time.

Basic Popovers

MAKES 8 POPOVERS

1 cup	all-purpose flour	250 mL
½ tsp	salt	2 mL
2	eggs	2
1 cup	milk	250 mL
1 tbsp	butter or margarine, melted (or shortening)	15 mL

TIP: If you don't have a popover pan, use eight ¾-cup (175 mL) custard cups.

- *Preheat oven to 425°F (220°C)*
- *Popover pan*

1. In a large bowl, sift together flour and salt. Make a well in the center.

2. In a medium bowl, whisk eggs, milk and melted butter until blended and smooth. Pour into the well in the flour mixture and whisk until batter is smooth.

3. Grease and flour 8 cups in the popover pan, two in each row. Spoon batter into prepared cups, filling each about half full. Fill the empty cups with about the same amount of cold water.

4. Bake in preheated oven for 35 minutes. Remove from oven, prick each popover in two or three places with a fork or a pointed knife to let steam escape and return to oven for 5 minutes, or until crisp, popped and a deep golden brown. Serve immediately.

Mom's Golden Popovers

MAKES 9 TO 10 POPOVERS

1 cup	all-purpose flour	250 mL
Pinch	salt	Pinch
3	eggs	3
1 cup	milk	250 mL

TIP: If you don't have a popover pan, use nine to ten ¾-cup (175 mL) custard cups.

- *Preheat oven to 450°F (230°C)*
- *2 popover pans*

1. In a large bowl, mix together flour and salt. Make a well in the center.

2. In a medium bowl, whisk together eggs and milk until blended and smooth. Pour into the well in the flour mixture and whisk just until blended.

3. Grease and flour 5 cups in one popover pan and 4 to 5 cups in the other. Spoon batter into prepared cups, filling about half full. Fill the empty cups with about the same amount of cold water.

4. Bake in preheated oven for 15 minutes. Reduce oven temperature to 350°F (180°C) and, without opening the oven door, bake for another 10 minutes. Remove from oven, prick each popover in two or three places with a fork or a pointed knife to let steam escape and return to oven for 5 minutes, or until firm and golden brown. Serve immediately.

Light Popovers

MAKES 6 POPOVERS

2	eggs	2
1 cup	all-purpose flour	250 mL
1 cup	milk	250 mL
½ tsp	salt	2 mL
1 tbsp	vegetable oil	15 mL

TIPS: If you don't have a popover pan, use six ¾-cup (175 mL) custard cups.

If you prefer popovers that are dry inside, leave popovers in turned-off oven, with door ajar, for about 30 minutes after they are finished baking.

- *Preheat oven to 475°F (230°C)*
- *Popover pan*

1. In a medium mixer bowl, beat eggs. Add flour, milk and salt and beat for 1 to 2 minutes. Add the oil and beat for another minute. Do not over-beat.

2. Grease and flour 6 alternating cups in the popover pan. Spoon batter into prepared cups, filling each about half full. Fill the empty cups with about the same amount of cold water.

3. Bake in preheated oven for 15 minutes, then reduce oven temperature to 350°F (180°C) and bake for another 25 minutes. Remove from oven, prick each popover in two or three places with a fork or a pointed knife to let steam escape and return to oven for 5 minutes, or until firm and golden brown. Serve immediately.

Popovers for Two

MAKES 4 POPOVERS

½ cup	all-purpose flour	125 mL
¼ tsp	salt	1 mL
2	eggs	2
½ cup	milk	125 mL

TIP: If you don't have a popover pan, use four ¾-cup (175 mL) custard cups.

- *Preheat oven to 425°F (220°C)*
- *Popover pan*

1. In a medium bowl, mix together flour and salt. Make a well in the center.
2. Add eggs and milk to the well in the flour mixture and whisk together just until blended.
3. Grease and flour 4 cups in the popover pan, one in each row. Spoon batter into prepared cups, filling each about half full. Fill the empty cups with about the same amount of cold water.
4. Bake in preheated oven for 20 minutes. Remove from oven, prick each popover in two or three places with a fork or a pointed knife to let steam escape and return to oven for 5 minutes, or until puffed and golden brown. Serve immediately.

Orange Popovers

MAKES 8 POPOVERS

4	eggs	4
1 cup	milk	250 mL
¾ cup	all-purpose flour	175 mL
¾ cup	whole wheat flour	175 mL
¼ cup	thawed frozen orange juice concentrate	50 mL
4 tsp	butter or margarine, melted	20 mL
½ tsp	salt	2 mL

TIP: If you don't have a popover pan, use eight ¾-cup (175 mL) custard cups.

- *Preheat oven to 450°F (230°C)*
- *Popover pan*

1. In a large bowl, whisk eggs and milk. Add flours, ¼ cup (50 mL) water, juice, melted butter and salt and whisk until well blended and smooth.
2. Grease and flour 8 cups in the popover pan, two in each row. Spoon batter into prepared cups, filling each about half full. Fill the empty cups with about the same amount of cold water.
3. Bake in preheated oven for 20 minutes, reduce oven temperature to 350°F (180°C) and bake for another 15 minutes. Remove from oven, prick each popover in two or three places with a fork or a pointed knife to let steam escape and return to oven for 5 minutes, or until puffy and golden brown. Serve warm.

Sweet Jam 'n' Butter Popovers

MAKES 12 POPOVERS

4	eggs	4
2 cups	milk	500 mL
2 cups	all-purpose flour	500 mL
2 tsp	granulated sugar	10 mL
1 tsp	salt	5 mL
1 tsp	grated orange zest	5 mL
½ tsp	ground nutmeg	2 mL

TIPS: If you don't have a popover pan, use twelve ¾-cup (175 mL) custard cups. These taste great with your favorite jam and butter, or with honey.

- *Preheat oven to 450°F (230°C)*
- *Popover pan, greased and floured*

1. In a large mixer bowl, beat eggs and milk until well blended. Add flour, sugar, salt, zest and nutmeg and beat just until well blended.

2. Spoon batter into prepared popover pan, filling each cup about half full.

3. Bake in preheated oven for 15 minutes, then reduce oven temperature to 350°F (180°C) and bake for another 15 minutes. Remove from oven, prick each popover in two or three places with a fork or a pointed knife to let steam escape and return to oven for 5 minutes, or until puffed and golden brown. Serve immediately.

Cheesy Breakfast Popovers

MAKES 8 POPOVERS

1 cup	all-purpose flour	250 mL
½ tsp	salt	2 mL
2	eggs	2
1 cup	milk	250 mL
½ cup	shredded Cheddar or Gouda cheese (about 2 oz/60 g)	125 mL

TIPS: If you don't have a popover pan, use eight ¾-cup (175 mL) custard cups. These popovers are delicious alone or with scrambled eggs.

- *Preheat oven to 450°F (230°C)*
- *Popover pan*

1. In a large bowl, mix together flour and salt. Make a well in the center.

2. In a small bowl, whisk eggs and milk until frothy. Pour into the well in the flour mixture and whisk just until blended. Do not over-beat. Add cheese and stir until well mixed.

3. Grease and flour 8 cups in the popover pan, two in each row. Spoon batter into prepared cups, filling each about half full. Fill the empty cups with about the same amount of cold water.

4. Bake in preheated oven for 25 minutes. Remove from oven, prick each popover in two or three places with a fork or a pointed knife to let steam escape and return to oven for 5 minutes, or until puffed and golden brown. Serve immediately.

Sage Butter Popovers

MAKES 6 POPOVERS

1 1/4 cups	all-purpose flour	300 mL
1/2 tsp	crumbled dried sage leaves	2 mL
1/4 tsp	salt	1 mL
1/4 tsp	ground black pepper	1 mL
3	eggs	3
1 1/4 cups	milk, at room temperature	300 mL

Sage Butter

1/2 cup	butter, softened	125 mL
1/2 tsp	crumbled dried sage leaves	2 mL
1/4 tsp	ground black pepper	1 mL

TIP: If you don't have a popover pan, use six 3/4-cup (175 mL) custard cups.

• *Preheat oven to 450°F (230°C)*
• *Popover pan*

1. In a large bowl, combine flour, sage, salt and pepper. Make a well in the center.

2. In a medium bowl, whisk eggs and milk until frothy and pale in color, about 2 minutes. Pour into the well in the flour mixture and stir just until blended.

3. Grease and flour 6 alternating cups in the popover pan. Spoon batter into prepared cups, filling each about half full. Fill the empty cups with about the same amount of cold water.

4. Bake in preheated oven for 15 minutes, then reduce heat to 350°F (180°C) and bake for another 25 minutes. Remove from oven, prick each popover in two or three places with a fork or a pointed knife to let steam escape and return to oven for 5 minutes, or until puffed and golden brown.

5. *Prepare sage butter:* In a small mixer bowl, combine butter, sage and pepper, beating on low speed until light and fluffy.

6. Serve hot popovers with sage butter.

Turnovers

Easy Apple Spice Turnovers

MAKES 12 TURNOVERS

1	package (double crust) piecrust mix	1
1	can (19 oz/540 mL) pie-sliced apples, drained	1
3 tbsp	brown sugar	45 mL
½ tsp	ground allspice	2 mL
	Vegetable oil for frying	
	Sifted confectioner's (icing) sugar	

- *Large frying pan or deep fryer*

1. Prepare piecrust mix according to package instructions. Divide dough in half. Roll out each half on a floured work surface to ¼-inch (0.5 cm) thickness. Cut out 12 rounds with a 4-inch (10 cm) cookie cutter.

2. In a medium bowl, combine apples, brown sugar and allspice and toss together to coat. Spread 2 tbsp (25 mL) of this apple mixture over half of each pastry round, fold the other half of the round evenly over the filling half and press all around the edges with a fork to seal.

3. Pour oil into frying pan or fryer, about 1 inch (2.5 cm) deep, and bring to medium heat or to 350°F (180°C). Drop turnovers one at a time into the hot fat and cook for about 5 minutes, turning often, until golden brown. Remove from pan, drain well on paper towel and let cool slightly. Dust with confectioner's sugar and serve while still warm.

Apple Cinnamon Turnovers

MAKES 24 TURNOVERS

24	wonton wrappers	24
2	medium apples, peeled, cored and finely diced	2
1 tbsp	brown sugar	15 mL
1 tsp	ground cinnamon	5 mL
1 tsp	freshly squeezed lemon juice	5 mL
	Sifted confectioner's (icing) sugar (optional)	

- *Preheat oven to 350°F (180°C)*
- *Large baking sheet, lightly greased*

1. Place wonton wrappers on a flat work surface.

2. In a medium bowl, toss together apples, brown sugar, cinnamon and lemon juice, until well blended. Drop by teaspoonfuls onto center of each wrapper. Wet your fingers with water and moisten the edges of wrappers. Fold one corner over filling to make a triangle and press sides together firmly with your fingers or a fork to seal.

3. Place turnovers on prepared baking sheet and bake in preheated oven for 15 to 20 minutes, or until golden brown. Place on serving plate to cool slightly and dust with confectioner's sugar, if desired.

Apple Cream Cheese Turnovers

MAKES 24 TURNOVERS

¾ cup	butter or margarine, softened	175 mL
1	package (8 oz/250 g) cream cheese, softened	1
1	egg, separated	1
2 cups	all-purpose flour	500 mL
6	medium apples, peeled, cored and thinly sliced	6
⅔ cup	granulated sugar	150 mL
2 tsp	ground cinnamon	10 mL
	Additional granulated sugar (optional)	

- *2 baking sheets, greased*

1. In a large mixer bowl, cream butter and cream cheese until soft and smooth.

2. In a small bowl, whisk egg yolk (refrigerate the egg white) and 2 tbsp (25 ml) cold water and add to creamed mixture. Gradually add flour and beat until well blended. Shape dough into a ball, wrap in plastic wrap and chill in refrigerator for about 1 hour. Meanwhile, preheat the oven to 375°F (190°C).

3. In a medium saucepan, over medium-high heat, combine apples, sugar and cinnamon, toss together and bring to a boil. Lower heat to low, cover and simmer for about 10 minutes, or until apples are tender. Remove from heat.

4. Roll out pastry on a floured work surface to ⅛-inch (2.5 mm) thickness. Cut out 24 rounds with a 4-inch (10 cm) cookie cutter. Place 2 tbsp (25 mL) of apple mixture on half of each circle. Brush around the edges with water and then fold pastry over filling and press around edges with a fork to seal.

5. In a small bowl, whisk egg white and 1 tbsp (15 mL) of water and brush over each turnover. Sprinkle granulated sugar over tops, if desired.

6. Place 12 turnovers on each prepared baking sheet and bake in preheated oven for 20 to 25 minutes, or until golden brown. Cool on wire racks.

Raspberry Turnovers

MAKES 12 TURNOVERS

1	sheet or block frozen puff pastry, thawed (about 8.5 oz/255 g)	1
¾ cup	red raspberry jam	175 mL
1	egg, lightly beaten	1
	Granulated sugar	

TIP: To make a puffy, crisp turnover, use French pastry.

- *Preheat oven to 450°F (230°C)*
- *Baking sheet, ungreased*

1. Unfold pastry and roll out to a rectangle 15 inches (38 cm) wide and 20 inches (50 cm) long. Cut lengthwise into 3 pieces, then crosswise into 4 pieces, making twelve 5-inch (12.5 cm) squares in all.
2. Place 1 tbsp (15 mL) jam in the middle of each square and brush the edges with beaten egg. Fold dough over, making triangles, and press down on the edges with your thumb or a fork to seal. Brush tops with the remaining egg and place turnovers on baking sheet.
3. Bake in preheated oven for 15 minutes, then reduce oven temperature to 350°F (180°C) and bake for 25 to 30 minutes more, or until tops are golden brown. Sprinkle with sugar.

Strawberry Mock Turnovers

MAKES 12 TURNOVERS

2 cups	hulled, washed and chopped fresh strawberries (about 12 oz/375 g)	500 mL
6 to 8 tbsp	strawberry preserves	90 to 120 mL
	Grated zest of 1 lemon	
12	slices soft white sandwich bread	12
⅓ cup + 1 tbsp	butter or margarine, melted	90 mL
	Sifted confectioner's (icing) sugar (optional)	

TIP: I use the same bread slices and method to make mock blintzes, replacing the strawberry filling with cottage cheese filling, or any other blintz filling.

- *Preheat oven to 400°F (200°C)*
- *Baking sheet, lightly greased*

1. In a medium bowl, mix together strawberries, preserves and zest until well blended.
2. Remove crusts from bread slices and flatten each slice with a rolling pin. Spoon 1 tbsp (15 mL) strawberry mixture in the center of each flattened slice of bread and fold over to form a triangle. Brush both sides of each turnover with the melted butter and place turnovers on prepared baking sheet.
3. Bake in preheated oven for about 5 minutes, then turn over and bake for another 5 to 6 minutes, or until golden brown. Cool on wire rack and dust with confectioner's sugar, if desired.

Apple Cream Cheese Turnovers (page 63) ➤

Jam and Nut Half Moons

MAKES ABOUT
5 DOZEN TURNOVERS

1 cup	jam (your favorite, apricot, berry or other)	250 mL
¾ cup	chopped nuts (walnuts or other)	175 mL
½ cup	raisins	125 mL
3	eggs	3
¾ cup	granulated sugar	175 mL
½ cup	shortening, softened	125 mL
½ cup	milk	125 mL
	Grated zest of 1 orange and 1 lemon	
¼ cup	freshly squeezed orange juice	50 mL
¼ cup	freshly squeezed lemon juice	50 mL
1 tsp	vanilla	5 mL
4½ cups	all-purpose flour (approx.)	1.125 L
2 tsp	baking powder	10 mL
	Sifted confectioner's (icing) sugar (optional)	

TIP: For a vanilla icing, use 1 cup (250 mL) of confectioner's (icing) sugar and 4 tsp (20 mL) of water, mixing until smooth. If a chocolate icing is desired, add about 1 tbsp (15 mL) of unsweetened cocoa powder to the vanilla icing. Drizzle half moons with either or both.

- *Preheat oven to 350°F (180°C)*
- *Baking sheet, ungreased*

1. In a small bowl, mix together jam, nuts and raisins and set aside.

2. In a large mixer bowl, beat eggs and sugar until light and fluffy. Add shortening and beat until well blended and smooth. Add milk, zests, juices and vanilla and beat until thoroughly blended. Slowly beat in about half of the flour, then the baking powder. Stir in remaining flour with a wooden spoon, or your hands, until a soft dough forms. If dough is a bit sticky, add a few tablespoons of flour until the right consistency.

3. Place dough on a floured work surface and tear off evenly sized pieces, about 1½ inches (4 cm) each, and roll each out into a 4-inch (10 cm) round. Use a 4-inch (10 cm) cookie cutter to trim each, if you want an exact measurement.

4. Spread a rounded teaspoon of the jam mixture over one half of each round, but not to the edges, then fold over opposite half so that edges meet, like a half moon. Press down with your fingers or crimp with a fork to seal. Place half moons on baking sheet.

5. Bake in preheated oven for 25 to 30 minutes, or until golden brown. Cool on wire rack. Sprinkle with confectioner's sugar, if desired.

Apricot Turnovers

MAKES 10 TURNOVERS

1	package (8 oz/250 g) cream cheese, softened	1
½ cup	apricot jam	125 mL
10	slices white sandwich bread, crusts removed	10
	Milk or light (5%) cream	
	Granulated sugar	
	Flaked coconut (optional)	

- *Preheat oven to 400°F (200°C)*
- *Baking sheet, lightly greased*

1. In a small bowl, mix together cream cheese and jam until blended.
2. Spread 2 tbsp (25 mL) of this mixture on each slice of bread and fold each slice diagonally. Press edges together firmly with fingers or a fork to seal well.
3. Place turnovers on prepared baking sheet, brush each with milk and sprinkle with sugar and coconut, if desired.
4. Bake in preheated oven for 10 to 12 minutes, or until golden brown.

Tempting Sweet Potato Turnovers

MAKES 12 TURNOVERS

2½ cups	all-purpose flour	625 mL
1 tsp	baking powder	5 mL
½ tsp	salt	2 mL
¾ cup	butter-flavored shortening	175 mL
Filling		
1	can (19 oz/540 mL) crushed pineapple, drained	1
2 cups	mashed sweet potatoes (no butter or milk added)	500 mL
1¼ cups	granulated sugar	300 mL
1 tsp	grated lemon zest	5 mL
1 tsp	grated orange zest	5 mL
½ tsp	ground cinnamon	2 mL
¼ tsp	ground allspice	1 mL
¼ tsp	ground ginger (optional)	1 mL
	Milk	
	Granulated sugar	

- *Preheat oven to 425°F (220°C)*
- *2 baking sheets, greased*

1. In a medium bowl, combine flour, baking powder and salt. Cut in shortening with a pastry blender or two knives until mixture resembles coarse crumbs. Add 6 tbsp (90 mL) cold water, 1 tbsp (15 mL) at a time, stirring until a ball of soft dough forms.
2. Place dough on a floured work surface and divide into 12 pieces. Roll each piece into a 6-inch (15 cm) circle.
3. *Prepare filling:* In a large saucepan, over low heat, combine pineapple, sweet potatoes, sugar, zests, cinnamon, allspice and ginger and cook, stirring, until thickened, about 10 to 12 minutes. Set aside to cool.
4. Place ¼ cup (50 mL) of cooled filling onto half of each circle. Fold dough over filling and press edges with your fingers or a fork to seal. Place turnovers onto prepared baking sheets. Brush with some milk and sprinkle with granulated sugar. Cut slits in tops to allow steam to escape.
5. Bake in preheated oven for 15 to 20 minutes, or until golden brown. Serve hot or warm with a meal.

Mini Chocolate Puff Turnovers

MAKES 9 MINI TURNOVERS

1	sheet or block frozen puff pastry, thawed (about 8.5 oz/255 g)	1
4	squares (each 1 oz/30 g) semi-sweet baking chocolate, broken into chunks	4
1	egg, lightly beaten	1
	Sifted confectioner's (icing) sugar	

TIP: This recipe calls for 1 sheet of puff pastry. Because a package of puff pastry contains many sheets, use as many as you like and adjust the amount of chocolate accordingly.

- *Preheat oven to 425°F (220°C)*
- *Baking sheet, lightly greased*

1. Place the puff pastry on a floured work surface and trim or roll into a 9-inch (23 cm) square. Cut sheet into nine 3-inch (7.5 cm) squares.

2. Place a chunk of chocolate near one corner, brush two sides of the square with some of the egg and then fold dough over diagonally to cover the chocolate chunk. Pinch edges with your fingers or a fork to seal and place turnovers on prepared baking sheet. Brush tops with the remaining egg.

3. Bake in preheated oven for 10 to 15 minutes, or until golden brown. Cool slightly, then dust with confectioner's sugar.

Special Breakfast Turnovers

MAKES ABOUT 2 DOZEN TURNOVERS

1	package (4 oz/125 g) cream cheese, softened	1
1	egg yolk	1
⅓ cup	peach preserves	75 mL
2 cups	all-purpose flour	500 mL
1 tbsp	granulated sugar	15 mL
1 tbsp	baking powder	15 mL
½ tsp	cream of tartar	2 mL
¼ tsp	salt	1 mL
½ cup	butter or margarine	125 mL
¾ cup	milk or light (5%) cream	175 mL

- *Preheat oven to 450°F (230°C)*
- *Baking sheet, lightly greased*

1. In a small mixer bowl, beat cream cheese and egg yolk until softened and smooth. Stir in peach preserves and mix to blend.

2. In a large bowl, combine flour, sugar, baking powder, cream of tartar and salt. Mix well and then cut in butter until mixture resembles coarse crumbs. Add the milk and stir with a fork until mixture is just blended and moistened. Place dough on a lightly floured surface and knead gently until the dough is nearly smooth. Cut in half and roll out one half to ⅛-inch (0.25 cm) thickness and cut into circles with a 4-inch (10 cm) cookie cutter, rerolling scraps.

3. Place a heaping teaspoonful (5 mL) of cream cheese filling onto the center of each circle. Brush the edge of one half of each circle with water then fold over opposite side to form a half moon. Press edges with a fork to seal, and make two small slits in each. Repeat with remaining dough and filling.

4. Place turnovers on prepared baking sheet and bake in preheated oven for 10 to 15 minutes, or until golden brown. Cool slightly on wire rack, then serve warm.

Mushroom and Broccoli Turnovers

MAKES 4 DOZEN TURNOVERS

⅓ cup	butter or margarine, softened	75 mL
1	package (8 oz/250 g) cream cheese, softened	1
1 cup	all-purpose flour	250 mL
2½ cups	small broccoli florets	625 mL
1½ cups	finely chopped fresh mushrooms	375 mL
1½ cups	shredded old Cheddar cheese (about 6 oz/175 g)	375 mL
¼ cup	Dijon mustard	50 mL
	Ground nutmeg	
	Pepper	
1	egg, lightly beaten, mixed with 1 tbsp (15 mL) water	1

- *Baking sheet, greased*

1. In a large mixer bowl, on medium speed, cream butter and cream cheese, beating until softened and blended. Add flour and beat until a soft dough forms. Divide dough in half, form into two balls and cover each with plastic wrap. Chill in refrigerator for 1 to 2 hours. Meanwhile, preheat oven to 400°F (200°C).

2. In a large saucepan, blanch broccoli in boiling water for 2 minutes. Drain well and place on paper towels, patting dry and then chopping florets.

3. In a large bowl, combine the chopped broccoli, mushrooms and cheese. Season to taste with nutmeg and pepper.

4. On a well floured work surface, roll out each portion of dough to ⅛ inch (2.5 mm) thickness. Cut out circles with a 3-inch (7.5 cm) cookie cutter, rerolling scraps. Spread mustard on each circle, leaving a ½-inch (1 cm) border around the edges. Place a teaspoonful (5 mL) of broccoli mixture onto one side of each circle.

5. Brush egg-water wash around the edges of each circle. Fold each in half and press down with a fork to seal. Make two small slits in each to allow steam to escape. Brush tops with remaining egg mixture. Repeat with remaining dough and filling.

6. Place turnovers on baking sheet and bake in preheated oven for 15 to 20 minutes, or until golden brown. Cool slightly on wire rack and serve warm.

Spinach Feta Turnovers

**MAKES ABOUT
9 DOZEN TURNOVERS**

36	frozen phyllo sheets, thawed (about 1½ packages, each 16 oz/454 g)	36
2	eggs, lightly beaten	2
1	package (10 oz/284 g) fresh spinach, chopped	1
¾ cup	feta cheese, finely crumbled (about 6 oz/175 g)	175 mL
¼ cup	chopped fresh dill (optional)	50 mL
2 tsp	dried onion flakes	10 mL
¼ tsp	ground black pepper	1 mL
¼ cup	butter or margarine, melted	50 mL

- *Preheat oven to 375°F (190°C)*
- *Baking sheet, lightly greased*

1. Place phyllo sheets on a work surface and cover with a damp tea towel to prevent them from drying out.
2. In a large bowl, whisk eggs. Mix in spinach, cheese, dill (if using), onion and pepper.
3. Stack two sheets of phyllo dough together. Cut crosswise into 6 strips about 3 inches (7.5 cm) wide. With a pastry brush, lightly brush each strip with melted butter. Spoon 1 tsp (5 mL) spinach filling about 1 inch (2.5 cm) away from bottom of each strip. Fold one bottom corner over filling to form a triangle. Fold in this manner to end of strip, folding end flap underneath. Brush tops with more of the melted butter. Cut a small slit in the top of each. Repeat with more sheets of phyllo dough until all the spinach filling is used up.
4. Place turnovers on prepared baking sheet and bake in preheated oven for 10 to 15 minutes, or until tops are golden brown. Serve hot.

Puffy Turkey Turnovers

MAKES 8 TURNOVERS

1½ cups	cubed cooked turkey (about 1 lb/500 g)	375 mL
⅔ cup	shredded Swiss cheese (about 4 oz/125 g)	150 mL
3 tbsp	Dijon mustard	45 mL
1	package (14 oz/397 g) frozen puff pastry, thawed	1
1	egg, lightly beaten	1
1 tbsp	milk	15 mL

- *Preheat oven to 375°F (190°C)*
- *2 baking sheets, greased or lined with parchment paper*

1. In a large bowl, combine turkey, cheese and mustard and mix together to blend.
2. On a lightly floured surface, roll out half of the pastry to a 9-inch (23 cm) square, then cut into 4 squares. Repeat with the other half. Place ¼ cup (50 mL) of the turkey mixture in the center of each square.
3. In a small bowl, whisk egg and milk. Brush over edges of squares. Fold in half diagonally to form a triangle and press down on edges with a fork to seal. Place on prepared baking sheets. Brush lightly with remaining egg mixture.
4. Bake in preheated oven for 25 to 30 minutes, or until tops are golden brown.

Bacon Turnovers

MAKES 25 TO 30 TURNOVERS

½ lb	sliced bacon	250 g
1	large onion, diced	1
3	envelopes (each ¼ oz/7 g) active dry yeast	3
½ cup	warm water	125 mL
1 cup	warm milk	250 mL
½ cup	butter or margarine, melted	125 mL
1½ tsp	salt	7 mL
1	egg, lightly beaten	1

- *Preheat oven to 425°F (220°C)*
- *Baking sheet, greased*

1. In a skillet, cook bacon until well done. Transfer to a medium bowl, crumble bacon, add onion and mix together. Set aside.

2. In a large mixer bowl, dissolve yeast in the warm water. Add milk, butter and salt and beat until blended and smooth and a soft dough is formed. Place dough on a floured work surface and knead for 5 to 6 minutes, or until smooth and elastic. Transfer dough to a greased bowl and turn once so that top is also greased. Cover and set aside in a warm place to rise for about 25 to 30 minutes, or until double in size, then punch dough down and place on floured work surface again.

3. Cut dough into 25 to 30 pieces. Take each piece and roll it out into a circle, 3 inches (7.5 cm) in diameter if you want mini turnovers, or 4 inches (10 cm) for a regular turnover. Put 1½ to 2 tsp (7 to 10 mL) of the bacon mixture on one side of each circle. Fold dough over the filling and press down on edges with your fingers or a fork to seal.

4. Place turnovers onto prepared baking sheet, leaving room between each. Cover with a towel and let rise in a warm place until double in size, about 15 to 20 minutes. Brush tops of each with the beaten egg.

5. Bake in preheated oven for 10 to 15 minutes, or until golden brown. Cool slightly, but best when served warm.

Scones

Old-Fashioned Scones

MAKES 16 SCONES

2 cups	all-purpose flour	500 mL
1/2 cup	granulated sugar	125 mL
1 tsp	cream of tartar	5 mL
1/2 tsp	salt	2 mL
1/2 tsp	baking soda	2 mL
1/4 cup	shortening or butter	50 mL
1	egg	1
1/2 cup	milk	125 mL
1 tsp	vanilla	5 mL
3/4 cup	raisins (optional)	175 mL
	Additional milk and granulated sugar	

TIP: Serve these delicious scones warm, with butter, jam or cream cheese — or all three!

- *Preheat oven to 400°F (200°C)*
- *Baking sheet, ungreased*

1. In a large bowl, combine flour, sugar, cream of tartar, salt and baking soda. Cut in shortening with a pastry blender or two knives until mixture resembles coarse crumbs.

2. In a small bowl, whisk egg, milk and vanilla until blended. Pour into flour mixture and stir until mixture forms a dough. Fold in raisins, if desired.

3. Place dough on a floured work surface and divide into 4 portions. Place each portion on baking sheet and pat down with the palm of your hand. With a knife, score an X into each round to mark out 4 wedges.

4. Brush each portion with milk and sprinkle with sugar. Bake in preheated oven for 15 to 20 minutes, or until golden brown. Cool on wire rack and cut into wedges as marked.

Cheese 'n' Apple Scones

MAKES 8 SCONES

1 cup	shredded Cheddar cheese (about 4 oz/125 g)	250 mL
1 cup	peeled, cored and diced apples (about 1 medium)	250 mL
1 3/4 cups	all-purpose flour	425 mL
2 tbsp	granulated sugar	25 mL
1 1/2 tsp	baking powder	7 mL
1/2 tsp	salt	2 mL
1/4 tsp	baking soda	1 mL
1/3 cup	butter or margarine, cold	75 mL
1 cup	buttermilk	250 mL

- *Preheat oven to 450°F (230°C)*
- *Baking sheet, greased*

1. In a medium bowl, mix together cheese and apples to blend.

2. In a large bowl, combine flour, sugar, baking powder, salt and baking soda. Cut in butter with a pastry blender or two knives until mixture resembles coarse crumbs. Add buttermilk and mix together just until blended and moistened. Fold in the cheese-apple mixture.

3. Place dough on a floured work surface and knead 10 times. With the palm of your hand, pat dough into a 9-inch (23 cm) circle, then cut circle into 8 wedges. Separate the wedges and place them on the prepared baking sheet.

4. Bake in preheated oven for 15 minutes, or until golden brown. Cool slightly on wire rack and serve warm.

Giant Filled Apricot Scone

SERVES 12 OR 16

2	eggs	2
¼ cup	sour cream	50 mL
1 tbsp	milk	15 mL
⅔ cup	finely chopped dried apricots (about 4 oz/125 g)	150 mL
½ cup	quick-cooking rolled oats	125 mL
1½ cups	all-purpose flour	375 mL
¼ cup	granulated sugar	50 mL
2½ tsp	baking powder	12 mL
¼ tsp	salt	1 mL
⅓ cup	cold butter or margarine, cut into cubes	75 mL
	Additional granulated sugar (optional)	

Filling

1 tbsp	quick-cooking rolled oats	15 mL
3 tbsp	brown sugar	45 mL
1 tbsp	butter or margarine, softened	15 mL

• *Preheat oven to 400°F (200°C)*
• *Baking sheet, greased*

1. In a small bowl, beat eggs. Set aside 1 tbsp (15 mL). Whisk in sour cream and milk. Stir in apricots and mix well.

2. In a large bowl, combine oats, flour, sugar, baking powder and salt. Mix well to blend. Cut in butter with a pastry blender or two knives until mixture resembles coarse crumbs. Pour in apricot mixture, mixing well until a dough forms.

3. *Prepare filling:* In another small bowl, mix together oats, brown sugar and butter until well combined.

4. Place dough on a floured work surface and knead 12 times. Divide dough in half. With the palm of your hand, pat each portion into an 8-inch (20 cm) circle. Place one circle onto prepared baking sheet and sprinkle filling evenly over top. Place second circle over the filling and brush top with the reserved beaten egg. Sprinkle sugar over top, if desired. Using the point of a sharp knife, mark out 6 or 8 wedges, but do not cut.

5. Bake in preheated oven for 15 to 20 minutes, or until top is golden brown. Cool slightly on wire rack until warm. When ready to serve, follow markings and cut into wedges.

Chocolate Chip Banana Scones

MAKES 8 SCONES

2 cups	all-purpose flour	500 mL
2/3 cup	granulated sugar	150 mL
1/2 cup	chocolate chips (about 3 oz/90 g)	125 mL
1 tbsp	baking powder	15 mL
1 tsp	salt	5 mL
1/2 cup	cold butter or margarine, cut into cubes	125 mL
1	egg	1
3/4 cup	whipping (35%) cream	175 mL
1	very ripe large banana, mashed well	1
	Additional granulated sugar (optional)	

- *Preheat oven to 425°F (220°C)*
- *9-inch (2.5 L) square baking dish or a baking sheet, greased*

1. In a large bowl, combine flour, sugar, chocolate chips, baking powder and salt. Mix well to blend. Cut in butter with a pastry blender or two knives until mixture resembles coarse crumbs.

2. In a medium bowl, whisk egg and cream until frothy. Add mashed banana and stir until well blended. Pour into flour mixture and mix just until blended, moistened and a soft dough forms.

3. Place dough on a floured work surface and, with the palm of your hand, pat into an 8-inch (20 cm) circle. Place onto prepared baking dish or sheet and sprinkle with additional sugar, if desired.

4. Bake in preheated oven for 15 to 20 minutes, or until golden brown. Cool slightly on wire rack and serve warm. Cut into 8 wedges.

Traditional Blueberry Scones

MAKES ABOUT 12 SCONES

2 1/4 cups	all-purpose flour	550 mL
1/2 cup	granulated sugar	125 mL
2 tsp	baking powder	10 mL
1/2 tsp	salt	2 mL
1/2 tsp	ground cinnamon	2 mL
1/4 tsp	ground ginger	1 mL
	Finely grated zest of 1 orange (optional)	
1/4 cup	cold butter, cut into cubes	50 mL
1 cup	half-and-half (10%) cream	250 mL
1 cup	fresh or frozen, well-drained blueberries (about 6 oz/175 g)	250 mL
1	egg, lightly beaten (optional)	1

- *Preheat oven to 375°F (190°C)*
- *Baking sheet, lightly greased*

1. In a large bowl, combine flour, sugar, baking powder, salt, cinnamon, ginger and zest, if using. Cut in butter with pastry blender or two knives until mixture resembles coarse crumbs.

2. In a medium bowl, mix together cream and blueberries and stir into flour mixture, mixing just until blended and a soft dough forms.

3. Place dough on a floured work surface, knead 10 to 12 times and roll out into a circle 1/2 inch (1 cm) thick. Use a 2-inch (5 cm) or 3-inch (7.5 cm) cookie cutter, or the top of a glass, floured, to cut out scones, rerolling scraps. Brush tops of scones with beaten egg, if desired.

4. Bake in preheated oven for 15 to 20 minutes, or until golden brown. Cool slightly on wire rack and serve warm.

Buttermilk Scones

MAKES 12 SCONES

2 cups	all-purpose flour	500 mL
¼ cup	granulated sugar	50 mL
1 tbsp	baking powder	15 mL
1 tsp	salt	5 mL
½ tsp	baking soda	2 mL
½ tsp	ground cinnamon (optional)	2 mL
¼ cup	cold butter or margarine	50 mL
2	eggs, lightly beaten	2
⅓ cup	buttermilk	75 mL

- *Preheat oven to 400°F (200°C)*
- *Baking sheet, greased*

1. In a large bowl, combine flour, sugar, baking powder, salt, baking soda and cinnamon. Mix well to blend. Cut in butter with a pastry blender or two knives until mixture resembles coarse crumbs.

2. In a small bowl, lightly whisk eggs and buttermilk just to blend. Sir into flour mixture until a soft dough forms.

3. Place dough on a floured work surface and knead lightly 5 times. Divide dough in half. With the palm of your hand, pat each portion into a 7-inch (18 cm) circle and cut each into 6 wedges.

4. Place wedges on prepared baking sheet and bake in preheated oven for 10 to 12 minutes, or until golden brown. Cool slightly on wire rack and serve warm.

Crusty Cheddar Cheese Scones

MAKES 12 SCONES

3 cups	all-purpose flour	750 mL
2 tbsp	granulated sugar	25 mL
4 tsp	baking powder	20 mL
½ tsp	baking soda	2 mL
½ tsp	salt	2 mL
½ cup	cold butter or margarine, cut into cubes	125 mL
2 cups	shredded Cheddar cheese (about 8 oz/250 g)	500 mL
1	egg	1
1 cup	milk	250 mL
1 tbsp	vinegar	15 mL

- *Preheat oven to 425°F (220°C)*
- *Baking sheet, greased*

1. In a large bowl, combine flour, sugar, baking powder, baking soda and salt. Mix together to blend. Cut in butter with a pastry blender or two knives until mixture resembles coarse crumbs. Stir in cheese and mix well.

2. In a small bowl, whisk together egg, milk and vinegar. Add to flour mixture and mix gently with a fork until blended and moistened.

3. Spoon into 12 mounds on prepared baking sheet, leaving 2 inches (5 cm) between each.

4. Bake in preheated oven for 15 to 18 minutes, or until golden brown. Cool slightly on wire rack and serve warm.

Chunky Chocolate Scones

MAKES ABOUT 8 TO 12 SCONES

2 cups	all-purpose flour	500 mL
¼ cup	granulated sugar	50 mL
1 tbsp	baking powder	15 mL
½ tsp	salt	2 mL
¼ tsp	ground nutmeg	1 mL
⅓ cup + 1 tbsp	cold butter or margarine, cut into chunks	90 mL
5	squares (each 1 oz/30 g) bittersweet baking chocolate, coarsely chopped into chunks	5
2	eggs	2
¼ cup	buttermilk	50 mL
2 tsp	vanilla	10 mL
	Beaten egg or milk, for glaze (optional)	

- *Preheat oven to 400°F (200°C)*
- *Baking sheet, lightly greased*

1. In a large bowl, combine flour, sugar, baking powder, salt and nutmeg and mix together to blend. Cut in butter with a pastry blender or two knives until mixture resembles coarse crumbs. Stir in chocolate chunks.

2. In a small bowl, whisk together eggs, buttermilk and vanilla. Add to flour mixture and stir just until blended and a soft dough forms.

3. Place dough on a floured work surface, knead 3 to 4 times and roll out into a circle about ¾ to 1 inch (1.5 to 2.5 cm) thick. Cut out 3-inch (7.5 cm) rounds with a cookie cutter and place rounds on prepared baking sheet, rerolling scraps. Brush tops with beaten egg, if desired, or leave plain.

4. Bake in preheated oven for 15 to 20 minutes, or until golden brown. Cool slightly on wire rack and serve warm.

Southern Cornmeal Scones

MAKES 6 TO 8 SCONES

1 cup	all-purpose flour	250 mL
½ cup	yellow cornmeal	125 mL
¼ cup	grated Parmesan cheese (about 1 oz/30 g)	50 mL
2 tsp	baking powder	10 mL
½ tsp	baking soda	2 mL
½ tsp	crumbled dried sage	2 mL
¼ tsp	salt	1 mL
¼ cup	cold butter or margarine	50 mL
¾ cup	buttermilk	175 mL
	Additional grated Parmesan cheese (optional)	

TIP: You can use ½ cup (125 mL) all-purpose flour and ½ cup (125 mL) whole wheat flour in this recipe in place of the 1 cup (250 mL) all-purpose flour.

- *Preheat oven to 425°F (220°C)*
- *Baking sheet, lightly greased*

1. In a large bowl, combine flour, cornmeal, cheese, baking powder, baking soda, sage and salt. Mix well to blend. Work in butter with your fingers or a pastry blender until mixture resembles coarse crumbs. Add buttermilk and stir until just blended and moistened and a soft dough is formed.

2. Place dough on a floured work surface, knead 10 times and place on prepared baking sheet. With the palm of your hand, pat down into a 6-inch (15 cm) circle. Score into 6 or 8 wedges with the point of a sharp knife, but do not cut through. Sprinkle tops with extra Parmesan cheese, if desired, or leave plain.

3. Bake in preheated oven for 20 minutes, or until golden brown. Cool slightly on wire rack, cut into wedges as marked and serve warm.

Cranberry Yogurt Scones

MAKES 8 SCONES

1¾ cups	all-purpose flour	425 mL
2 tsp	baking powder	10 mL
1 tsp	baking soda	5 mL
½ tsp	salt	2 mL
1 cup	fresh or frozen cranberries (about 4 oz/125 g)	250 mL
1½ cups	plain yogurt	375 mL
1 tbsp	vegetable oil	15 mL
2 tsp	grated lemon zest	10 mL
1 tsp	vanilla	5 mL

- *Preheat oven to 425°F (220°C)*
- *Baking sheet, lightly greased*

1. In a large bowl, combine flour, baking powder, baking soda and salt. Mix well to combine. Add cranberries and mix together. Make a well in the center.

2. In a medium bowl, combine yogurt, oil, zest and vanilla. Mix together to blend. Pour into the well in the flour mixture and stir with a fork until well combined and a soft dough forms.

3. Place dough on a floured work surface and knead 5 or 6 times, until dough holds together well. Roll into a circle ½ to ¾ inch (1 to 1.5 cm) thick. Cut into 8 wedges and place wedges on prepared baking sheet.

4. Bake in preheated oven for 15 to 18 minutes, or until golden brown. Cool slightly on wire rack and serve warm.

Traditional Cream Scones

MAKES 8 SCONES

2 cups	all-purpose flour	500 mL
2 tbsp	granulated sugar	25 mL
3 tsp	baking powder	15 mL
Pinch	salt	Pinch
¼ cup	shortening or butter	50 mL
2	eggs	2
½ cup	half-and-half (10%) cream	125 mL
	Additional granulated sugar (optional)	

TIP: These scones are popular in England, at tea time, served with clotted cream and strawberry jam.

- *Preheat oven to 450°F (230°C)*
- *Baking sheet, ungreased*

1. In a large bowl, combine flour, sugar, baking powder and salt. Cut in shortening with a pastry blender or your fingers until mixture resembles coarse crumbs.

2. Break eggs into a small bowl, reserving a little of the white. Whisk eggs and stir in the cream. Add to the flour mixture, stirring with a fork until a soft dough forms.

3. Place dough on a floured work surface, knead for about 30 seconds and roll into an oblong ¾ inch (1.5 cm) thick. Cut into triangles, or into diamonds by making diagonal cuts in one direction and then in the other direction. Mix the reserved egg white with 1 tsp (5 mL) water and brush over tops. Sprinkle with granulated sugar, if desired.

4. Bake in preheated oven for 12 to 15 minutes, or until golden brown. Cool slightly on wire rack and serve warm.

Festive Fruit Scones

MAKES 12 SCONES

2 cups	all-purpose flour	500 mL
3 tbsp	granulated sugar	45 mL
2 tsp	baking powder	10 mL
1/4 tsp	salt	1 mL
1/3 cup + 1 tbsp	cold butter or margarine, cut into small chunks	90 mL
1 cup	chopped dried fruit (about 5 oz/150 g)	250 mL
2	eggs	2
1/2 cup	buttermilk	125 mL
	Additional buttermilk	
	Brown sugar	

TIP: For the dried fruit, I use 1/2 cup (125 mL) dried cherries and 1/2 cup (125 mL) dried apricots.

- *Preheat oven to 400°F (200°C)*
- *Large baking sheet, lightly greased*

1. In a large bowl, combine flour, sugar, baking powder and salt and mix well. Cut in butter with a pastry blender or two knives until mixture resembles coarse crumbs. Stir in dried fruit and mix well.
2. In a small bowl, whisk eggs and buttermilk to blend. Pour into flour mixture, stirring with a fork just until combined and moistened and a soft dough forms.
3. Spoon into 12 mounds on prepared baking sheet, leaving about 2 inches (5 cm) between each. Brush with buttermilk and sprinkle with brown sugar.
4. Bake in preheated oven for 15 minutes, or until golden brown. Cool slightly on wire rack and serve warm.

Poppy Seed Orange Scones

MAKES ABOUT 16 SCONES

2 cups	all-purpose flour	500 mL
1/4 cup	granulated sugar	50 mL
1 tbsp	baking powder	15 mL
1/2 tsp	salt	2 mL
1/4 cup	cold butter or margarine, cut into small cubes	50 mL
1/4 cup	poppy seeds	50 mL
	Finely grated zest of 1 orange	
1	egg	1
2/3 cup	half-and-half (10%) cream or milk	150 mL
	Additional granulated sugar (optional)	

- *Preheat oven to 375°F (190°C)*
- *Baking sheet, lightly greased*

1. In a large bowl, combine flour, sugar, baking powder and salt. Mix together to blend. Cut in butter, using a pastry blender or your fingertips, until mixture resembles coarse crumbs. Stir in poppy seeds and zest.
2. In a small bowl, whisk egg and cream until blended. Stir into flour mixture, mixing just until blended, moistened and a soft dough forms. Form dough into a ball.
3. Place ball of dough on a lightly floured work surface, knead about 10 times and roll out to a circle 1/2 inch (1 cm) thick. Cut out rounds with a 2-inch (5 cm) round cookie cutter or an inverted glass and place on prepared baking sheet, rerolling scraps. Sprinkle with the additional sugar, if desired.
4. Bake in preheated oven for 15 to 18 minutes, or until golden brown. Cool slightly on wire rack and serve warm.

Onion-Topped Herb Scones

MAKES 8 SCONES

2 tbsp	butter or margarine	25 mL
2	medium onions, thinly sliced	2
¾ tsp	dried thyme, divided	3 mL
1¾ cups	all-purpose flour (or half all-purpose and half whole wheat)	425 mL
1 tbsp	granulated sugar	15 mL
1 tbsp	chopped chives or green onion	15 mL
1 tbsp	chopped fresh parsley	15 mL
½ tsp	salt	2 mL
¼ cup	cold butter, cut into chunks	50 mL
1 cup	plain yogurt	250 mL

- *Preheat oven to 425°F (220°C)*
- *Baking sheet, lightly greased*

1. In a skillet, over medium heat, melt butter and add onions, cooking about 5 minutes, until tender. Stir in ¼ tsp (1 mL) of the thyme and cook for 1 to 2 minutes more. Remove from heat and set aside.

2. In a large bowl, combine flour, sugar, chives, parsley, salt and the remaining ½ tsp (10 mL) thyme. Mix together and then cut in butter, using your fingers or a pastry blender, until mixture resembles coarse crumbs. Stir in yogurt and, with a fork, mix until blended and moistened and a soft dough forms.

3. Place dough on a floured work surface and knead 5 to 6 times, until smooth. With the palm of your hand, pat down to an 8-inch (20 cm) circle about 1 inch (2.5 cm) thick. Score 8 wedges on surface of dough. Spread the reserved onion mixture evenly over top.

4. Bake in preheated oven for 20 minutes, or until golden brown. Cool slightly on wire rack, cut into wedges as marked and serve warm.

Oatmeal Scones

MAKES 8 SCONES

1½ cups	all-purpose flour	375 mL
1 cup	old-fashioned rolled oats	250 mL
½ tsp	salt	2 mL
¼ cup	butter or margarine, softened	50 mL
¾ cup	buttermilk	175 mL

TIP: Serve hot or warm, with butter, jam or honey.

- *Preheat oven to 400°F (200°C)*
- *Baking sheet, greased*

1. In a large bowl, combine flour, oats and salt. Mix well to blend. Cut in butter with a pastry blender or two knives until mixture resembles coarse crumbs. Stir in buttermilk, mixing just until blended and moistened and a soft dough is formed.

2. Place dough on a floured work surface and knead lightly a few times. Divide dough in half and roll each half into a circle ½ inch (1 cm) thick. Place on prepared baking sheet.

3. Bake in preheated oven for 12 to 15 minutes, or until golden brown. Cool slightly on wire rack and then cut each circle into 4 wedges.

Glazed Lemon Scones

MAKES 8 TO 12 SCONES

2 cups	all-purpose flour	500 mL
¼ cup	granulated sugar	50 mL
4 tsp	baking powder	20 mL
½ tsp	salt	2 mL
½ cup	butter or shortening	125 mL
1 tbsp	grated lemon zest	15 mL
1	egg	1
½ cup	milk	125 mL
¼ cup	freshly squeezed lemon juice	50 mL

Glaze

½ cup	confectioner's (icing) sugar, sifted	125 mL
4 tsp	freshly squeezed lemon juice	20 mL
	Yellow food coloring (about 3 to 4 drops, or as desired) (optional)	
	Grated lemon zest, for garnish	
	Slivered almonds, for garnish	

- *Preheat oven to 400°F (200°C)*
- *Baking sheet, ungreased*

1. In a large bowl, combine flour, sugar, baking powder and salt. Work in butter with your fingers or a pastry blender until mixture resembles coarse crumbs. Stir in lemon zest and blend.

2. In a small bowl, whisk egg, milk and lemon juice. Pour into flour mixture and mix until blended and moistened and a soft dough is formed.

3. Place dough on a floured work surface, knead 15 to 20 times and roll into a circle ¾ inch (1.5 cm) thick. Place on baking sheet. Score into 8 to 12 wedges with the point of a sharp knife.

4. Bake in preheated oven for 15 minutes, or until golden brown. Cool slightly on wire rack, cut into wedges as marked and serve warm.

5. *Prepare glaze:* In a small bowl, mix together confectioner's sugar and lemon juice. Add food coloring, if desired. Drizzle over warm scones and sprinkle with zest and almonds.

Old-Time Scottish Scones

MAKES 8 SCONES

2 cups	all-purpose flour	500 mL
2 tsp	granulated sugar	10 mL
1½ tsp	baking powder	7 mL
¼ tsp	salt	1 mL
1½ tbsp	shortening	22 mL
1 cup	milk	250 mL
Pinch	baking soda	Pinch

TIP: Serve hot, split in half, with butter and your favorite jam.

- *Griddle, ungreased*

1. In a large bowl, sift together flour, sugar, baking powder and salt. Cut in shortening with a pastry blender or your fingers until mixture resembles coarse crumbs.

2. In a small bowl, mix together milk and baking soda. Pour into flour mixture and mix together with a fork until blended, moistened and a soft dough forms.

3. Turn out dough onto a floured work surface, knead lightly 5 to 6 times and roll into a circle about ½ inch (1 cm) thick. Cut into 8 wedges.

4. Bake on griddle, over medium heat, turning over to brown both sides. Turn each scone on edge to brown the edges.

Scrumptious Chocolate 'n' Orange Scones

MAKES 16 SCONES

3 cups	buttermilk pancake mix	750 mL
2 tbsp	grated orange zest	25 mL
1½ cups	whipping (35%) cream	375 mL
6 tbsp	unsweetened cocoa powder	90 mL
6 tbsp	chopped milk chocolate	90 mL

TIP: When serving, mix the chocolate and plain scones for a colorful plate or basket.

- *Preheat oven to 425°F (220°C)*
- *Baking sheet, ungreased*

1. In a large bowl, mix together pancake mix and zest. Gradually stir in cream, mixing to blend, just until moistened and a soft dough forms. Form into a ball and divide dough in half. Leave one portion as is; to the other portion add cocoa and mix into dough.

2. Place both chocolate and plain dough on a floured work surface. Gently knead 3 tbsp (45 mL) chopped chocolate into each portion of dough, kneading about 5 to 6 times. Roll out each portion to a circle ¾ inch (1.5 cm) thick. Cut out 8 rounds from each dough, using a 2-inch (5 cm) cookie cutter, rerolling scraps.

3. Place rounds about 1 inch (2.5 cm) apart on baking sheet and bake in preheated oven for 10 to 12 minutes, or until golden brown. Cool slightly on wire rack and serve warm.

Golden Tea Scones

MAKES ABOUT 12 SCONES

2 cups	all-purpose flour	500 mL
4 tsp	baking powder	20 mL
1 tbsp	granulated sugar	15 mL
½ tsp	salt	2 mL
2 tbsp	cold butter or shortening	25 mL
1 cup	cold milk	250 mL
1	egg, lightly beaten, mixed with 1 tbsp (15 mL) water (optional)	1

TIP: To dress up your scones, add to the crumbly mixture ½ cup (125 mL) chopped pecans or raisins, or ½ cup (125 mL) chopped candied cherries or any other dried fruit.

- *Preheat oven to 450°F (230°C)*
- *Baking sheet, buttered*

1. In a large bowl, sift together flour, baking powder, sugar and salt. Cut in butter with a pastry blender or two knives until mixture is crumbly. Add milk and mix with a fork until blended, moistened and a soft dough forms.

2. Place dough on a floured work surface and knead gently about 5 to 6 times. Roll out dough into a circle ½ inch (1 cm) thick and cut out rounds, using a 2-inch (5 cm) round cookie cutter, rerolling scraps. Place rounds onto prepared baking sheet. If desired, brush tops with egg wash.

3. Bake in preheated oven for 12 to 15 minutes, or until golden brown. Cool slightly on wire rack and serve warm.

Potato Scones

MAKES 16 SCONES

¾ cup	sour cream	175 mL
¼ cup	butter or margarine	50 mL
2 tbsp + 1 tsp	granulated sugar	25 mL + 5 mL
½ tsp	baking soda	2 mL
¼ tsp	ground mace	1 mL
½ cup	cold mashed potatoes	125 mL
1	envelope (¼ oz/7 g) active dry yeast	1
½ cup	lukewarm water	125 mL
3 cups	all-purpose flour, divided	750 mL
½ tsp	salt	2 mL

- *Baking sheet, floured*

1. In a medium saucepan, over low heat, scald sour cream (see tip, page 86). Add butter, the 2 tbsp (25 mL) sugar, baking soda and mace and stir just until blended. Remove from heat and stir in the mashed potatoes. Mix well.

2. In a large bowl, dissolve the yeast and 1 tsp (5 mL) sugar in the lukewarm water. Mix yeast into the creamed potato mixture and add 1½ cups (375 mL) of the flour. Sift the salt and the remaining flour and add to yeast mixture. Stir until well blended, moistened and a soft dough forms.

3. Place dough on a floured work surface and knead until smooth and elastic. Place dough into a greased bowl, cover with a towel or plastic wrap and allow to rise to double the size, about 45 minutes. Then punch down, cover and let rise for another 10 minutes.

4. Divide dough into 4 equal parts. Roll each out into a 9-inch (23 cm) circle. Dust each with flour and cut each into 4 triangular scones. Place well apart on prepared baking sheet, cover with a towel or plastic wrap and let rise, in a warm spot, for about 45 minutes. Meanwhile, preheat oven to 375°F (190°C).

5. Bake in preheated oven for 15 minutes, or until golden brown. Serve hot.

Spicy Pumpkin Scones

MAKES ABOUT 16 SCONES

2 cups	all-purpose flour	500 mL
1/2 cup	packed brown sugar	125 mL
2 tsp	baking powder	10 mL
1 tsp	ground cinnamon	5 mL
1/2 tsp	baking soda	2 mL
1/4 tsp	ground nutmeg	1 mL
1/4 tsp	ground allspice	1 mL
Pinch	salt	Pinch
1/4 cup	butter or margarine	50 mL
1/2 cup	raisins	125 mL
1	egg, lightly beaten	1
3/4 cup	canned pumpkin purée	175 mL
2 tbsp	buttermilk	25 mL
1	egg white, lightly beaten	1

- *Preheat oven to 400°F (200°C)*
- *Baking sheet, ungreased*

1. In a large bowl, combine flour, brown sugar, baking powder, cinnamon, baking soda, nutmeg, allspice and salt. Cut in butter with a pastry blender or two knives until mixture resembles coarse crumbs. Mix in raisins.

2. In a small bowl, mix egg, pumpkin and buttermilk. Add to flour mixture and mix until blended and a soft dough forms. Turn out dough onto a floured work surface and roll into a circle 3/4 inch (1.5 cm) thick. Cut out rounds using a 2-inch (5 cm) round cookie cutter or the top of an inverted glass and place on baking sheet, rerolling scraps.

3. Brush tops with the beaten egg white and bake in preheated oven for 12 to 15 minutes, or until golden brown. Cool slightly on wire rack and serve warm.

Sour Cream Scones

MAKES 16 SCONES

2 1/4 cups	cake flour	550 mL
1/4 cup	granulated sugar	50 mL
2 1/2 tsp	baking powder	12 mL
1/2 tsp	salt	2 mL
1/2 tsp	baking soda	2 mL
1	egg	1
1 cup	sour cream	250 mL
1/4 tsp	vanilla	1 mL

- *Preheat oven to 400°F (200°C)*
- *Baking sheet, ungreased*

1. In a large bowl, combine flour, sugar, baking powder, salt and baking soda, mixing until blended. Make a well in the center.

2. In a small bowl, whisk egg, sour cream and vanilla. Pour into the well in the flour mixture and stir with a fork until blended, just moistened and a soft dough is formed.

3. Turn out dough onto a floured work surface and knead gently about 5 to 10 times, working in a little more cake flour if the dough is too sticky. Divide dough in half and, with the palm of your hand, pat down each portion into a 6-inch (15 cm) circle about 1/2 inch (1 cm) in thickness. Cut each circle into 8 wedges and place wedges on baking sheet, leaving about 2 inches (5 cm) between each.

4. Bake in preheated oven for 15 minutes, or until golden brown. Cool slightly on wire rack and serve warm.

Super Raisin Nut Scones

MAKES 8 SCONES

2 cups	all-purpose flour	500 mL
½ cup	granulated sugar	125 mL
2 tsp	baking powder	10 mL
⅓ cup	butter or margarine	75 mL
2	eggs	2
¼ cup	milk or table (18%) cream	50 mL
½ cup	chopped nuts (pecans, hazelnuts, walnuts or other)	125 mL
½ cup	raisins	125 mL

TIP: Delicious when served with Maple Butter (see recipe, below).

- *Preheat oven to 375°F (190°C)*
- *Baking sheet, ungreased*

1. In a large bowl, combine flour, sugar and baking powder. Mix to blend and then cut in butter with a pastry blender or your fingertips until mixture resembles coarse crumbs.

2. In a small bowl, whisk eggs and milk and pour into flour mixture, stirring with a fork just until blended, moistened and a soft dough is formed. Stir in nuts and raisins and form dough into a ball.

3. Place dough on a floured work surface and cut into 8 portions. Shape each portion into a round ball and place on baking sheet. Using a sharp knife, slash an X in the center of each.

4. Bake in preheated oven for 15 minutes, or until golden brown. Cool slightly on wire rack and serve warm.

Super Maple Butter

½ cup	confectioner's (icing) sugar	125 mL
1 to 2 tsp	milk	5 to 10 mL
1 tsp	maple syrup	5 mL

1. In a small bowl, mix together sugar, milk and maple syrup and beat until smooth enough to spread.

Custards, Crème Brûlée & Flans

When baking custards, to minimize the possibility of curdling, place custard cups in a 13- by 9-inch (3 L) baking pan on the oven rack, then pour hot water into the pan until water reaches halfway up the cups. Then slide into oven and bake as directed. Do not over-bake, as custards will set as they cool. The point of a knife inserted in the center will come out clean when the custard is set and done.

A stirred custard is cooked in a double boiler over hot but not boiling water. Stir constantly.

When preparing crème brûlée, use light (5%) cream instead of milk, cool and chill, then broil for about 5 minutes until custard has a bubbly brown crust.

Perfect Baked Custard

SERVES 12

6	eggs, lightly beaten	6
2/3 cup	granulated sugar	150 mL
2 tsp	vanilla	10 mL
Pinch	salt	Pinch
5 cups	milk, scalded	1.25 L
	Ground cinnamon	
	Ground nutmeg	

TIPS: Milk, cream and sour cream are scalded when bubbles form around the edge of the pan.

If you put both pans in the oven at the same time, place them on different racks, and make sure one is not directly above the other. Put one on the right side of its rack and the other on the left.

This custard can be stored in the refrigerator, in the cups, covered with plastic wrap, for up to 1 week.

- *Preheat oven to 350°F (180°C)*
- *Twelve ¾-cup (175 mL) custard cups or ramekins*
- *Two 13- by 9-inch (3 L) baking pans*

1. In a large bowl, whisk together eggs, sugar, vanilla and salt. Gradually stir in milk, just until well blended. Spoon into custard cups. Sprinkle tops with cinnamon and nutmeg.

2. Place custard cups in baking pans set on oven racks. Pour hot water into each pan until it reaches halfway up the cups. Bake in preheated oven for 45 to 50 minutes, or until custard is set and a knife inserted near the center comes out clean. Remove cups to wire rack to cool. Serve warm or chilled.

Stirred Almond Custard

SERVES 8

6	egg yolks, lightly beaten	6
3 cups	milk	750 mL
1¼ cups	granulated sugar	300 mL
1½ tsp	unflavored gelatin powder, mixed with ⅓ cup (75 mL) milk	7 mL
1 tsp	vanilla	5 mL
1 tsp	almond extract	5 mL
2 cups	whipping (35%) cream, whipped	500 mL
1 to 2	bananas, sliced	1 to 2
½ cup	sliced almonds, toasted	125 mL

- *Double boiler*
- *Eight ¾-cup (175 mL) custard cups or ramekins*

1. In the top of a double boiler, over hot but not boiling water, combine egg yolks, milk and sugar. Cook over medium heat for 10 minutes, stirring constantly, until mixture thickens enough to coat the back of a metal spoon.

2. In a small saucepan, over low heat, heat the gelatin-milk mixture until gelatin is dissolved. Stir this mixture into the egg mixture and chill until partially set. Stir in vanilla and almond extract. Fold in the whipped cream and spoon into custard cups.

3. Chill in refrigerator until set, about 45 to 50 minutes. Garnish with banana slices and sprinkle with almonds.

Apple Custard Cups

SERVES 6

¾ cup	firmly packed brown sugar	175 mL
2 tbsp	butter or margarine, softened	25 mL
1 tsp	ground cinnamon	5 mL
6	medium baking apples, peeled and cored (leave whole)	6
2	eggs	2
2 cups	milk, scalded (see tip, opposite)	500 mL
⅓ cup	granulated sugar	75 mL
½ tsp	vanilla	2 mL
Pinch	salt	Pinch

- *Preheat oven to 350°F (180°C)*
- *Six ¾-cup (175 mL) custard cups or ramekins*
- *13- by 9-inch (3 L) baking pan*

1. In a small bowl, mix together brown sugar, butter and cinnamon.

2. Place the apples in the custard cups. Spoon the sugar mixture into the centers of the apples, dividing equally.

3. In a medium bowl, whisk eggs, milk, sugar, vanilla and salt until well blended. Spoon into each apple, dividing equally.

4. Place custard cups in baking pan set on oven rack and pour in hot water until it reaches halfway up the cups. Bake in preheated oven for 45 to 55 minutes, or until custard is set and a knife inserted in the center comes out clean. Remove cups to wire rack to cool. Serve warm or cool.

Banana Custard Pudding

SERVES 4

½ cup	granulated sugar	125 mL
1 tbsp	cornstarch	15 mL
Pinch	salt	Pinch
1½ cups	milk	375 mL
3	egg yolks, lightly beaten	3
1 tsp	vanilla	5 mL
1	firm medium banana, sliced	1
	Whipped topping (optional)	

1. In a medium saucepan, over medium heat, combine sugar, cornstarch and salt. Slowly add milk and bring to a boil, stirring constantly. Boil for about 2 minutes. Stir a small amount into the egg yolks and pour egg mixture back into saucepan. Continue cooking and stirring until mixture is thickened. Remove from heat and stir in vanilla.

2. Transfer to a medium glass bowl and chill in refrigerator for 1 hour. When ready to serve, fold in banana slices. Garnish with whipped topping and 1 or 2 banana slices, if desired.

Blueberry Custard

SERVES 4

1½ cups	half-and-half (10%) cream	375 mL
½ cup	granulated sugar	125 mL
2 tbsp	all-purpose flour	25 mL
1 tsp	grated lemon zest	5 mL
Pinch	salt	Pinch
3	egg yolks	3
2 tbsp	butter or margarine	25 mL
1 tbsp	vanilla	15 mL
1 tbsp	cornstarch	15 mL
1	can (16 oz/500 mL) blueberries, drained, juice reserved	1

1. In a medium saucepan, combine cream, sugar, flour, lemon zest and salt. Cook over medium heat and bring to a boil, stirring for about 2 to 3 minutes, until mixture becomes bubbly and thickened. Remove from heat.

2. In a small bowl, beat egg yolks lightly, then stir in a small amount of the hot mixture. Pour back into hot mixture and, over low heat, bring to a gentle boil, stirring constantly. Remove from heat and stir in butter and vanilla. Spoon into 4 individual custard cups or dessert dishes and set aside to cool.

3. In a small saucepan, over medium heat, cook cornstarch and reserved blueberry juice and bring to a boil. Stir for 2 minutes, or until mixture thickens. Spoon blueberries equally over custard, then spoon cornstarch mixture over top. Serve warm.

Velvety Chocolate Custard

SERVES 6

2 cups	milk	500 mL
½ cup	semi-sweet chocolate chips (about 3 oz/90 g)	125 mL
3	eggs, lightly beaten	3
¼ cup	granulated sugar	50 mL
1 tsp	vanilla	5 mL
Pinch	salt	Pinch

- *Preheat oven to 325°F (160°C)*
- *Six ⅔-cup (150 mL) custard cups or ramekins*
- *13- by 9-inch (3 L) baking pan*

1. In a medium saucepan, over low heat, cook milk and chocolate chips, stirring constantly until chocolate is melted. Set aside to cool slightly.

2. In a medium bowl, whisk together eggs, sugar, vanilla and salt. Gradually stir in the chocolate mixture. Pour into custard cups.

3. Place cups in baking pan set on oven rack and pour in hot water until it reaches halfway up the cups. Bake in preheated oven for 40 to 45 minutes, or until custard is set and a knife inserted near the center comes out clean. Remove cups to wire rack to cool. Invert onto serving dishes and garnish as desired.

Baked Coconut Custard

SERVES 6

4	eggs	4
⅓ cup	granulated sugar	75 mL
½ tsp	salt	2 mL
½ tsp	vanilla	2 mL
3 cups	milk	750 mL
1 cup	flaked coconut	250 mL
	Ground nutmeg	

TIP: Serve with your favorite sauce (see Sauces, pages 176–79).

- *Preheat oven to 325°F (160°C)*
- *Six ¾-cup (175 mL) custard cups or ramekins*
- *13- x 9-inch (3 L) baking pan*

1. In a large bowl, whisk eggs. Add sugar, salt and vanilla and blend well. Gradually add milk and mix well to incorporate. Stir in coconut. Spoon into custard cups, dividing equally. Sprinkle with nutmeg.

2. Place cups in baking pan set on oven rack and pour in boiling water until it reaches halfway up the cups. Bake in preheated oven for 35 to 40 minutes, or until custard is set and a knife inserted near the center comes out clean. Remove cups to wire rack to cool.

Honey Custard Cups

SERVES 6

3 cups	milk	750 mL
4	eggs	4
1/3 cup	liquid honey	75 mL
1 tsp	vanilla	5 mL
Pinch	salt	Pinch
	Ground nutmeg	

- *Preheat oven to 325°F (160°C)*
- *Six ¾-cup (175 mL) custard cups or ramekins*
- *13- x 9-inch (3 L) baking pan*

1. In a medium saucepan, on low heat, slowly scald milk (see tip, page 86). Remove from heat.

2. In a large bowl, whisk eggs. Add honey, vanilla and salt and whisk to incorporate. Stir in scalded milk until well blended. Strain mixture into a large measuring cup and pour into custard cups. Sprinkle nutmeg over top.

3. Place cups in baking pan set on wire rack and pour in boiling water until it reaches halfway up the cups. Bake in preheated oven for 35 to 40 minutes, or until custard is set and a knife inserted near the center comes out clean. Remove cups to wire rack to cool. Serve warm or chilled.

Cherry-Topped Lemon Custard Cake

SERVES 10 TO 12

1	angel food cake, either prepared or baked from a mix according to instructions	1
1	package (3.5 oz/102 g) instant lemon pudding mix	1
1½ cups	cold milk	375 mL
1 cup	sour cream	250 mL
1	can (19 oz/540 mL) cherry pie filling (or any other flavor)	1

- *13- by 9-inch (3 L) baking dish, ungreased*

1. Tear angel food cake into bite-size pieces and place in baking dish.

2. In a large mixer bowl, on medium speed, beat pudding mix, milk and sour cream for about 2 to 3 minutes, until thickened. Spread over cake in pan. Top with pie filling, spreading evenly. Chill for 1 to 2 hours, or until ready to serve.

Nectarine Custard

SERVES 8

3 cups	milk	750 mL
4 cups	peeled and thinly sliced ripe nectarines (about 4 medium)	1 L
3	eggs	3
3 tbsp	granulated sugar	45 mL
1 tsp	vanilla	5 mL
Pinch	salt	Pinch

- *Preheat oven to 325°F (160°C)*
- *Eight ¾-cup (175 mL) custard cups or ramekins*
- *13- x 9-inch (3 L) baking pan*

1. In a medium saucepan, scald milk (see tip, page 86). Remove from heat.
2. Spoon nectarine slices into custard cups, dividing equally.
3. In a large bowl, whisk eggs and stir in sugar, vanilla and salt. Slowly blend in scalded milk. Strain mixture over the nectarines, dividing equally.
4. Place cups in baking pan set on oven rack and pour in boiling water until it reaches halfway up the cups. Bake in preheated oven for 45 to 50 minutes, or until custard is set and a knife inserted near the center comes out clean. Remove cups to wire rack to cool. Serve warm or chilled.

Custard Pie

SERVES 6 TO 8

1	9-inch (23 cm) unbaked pastry shell	1
2½ cups	milk	625 mL
4	eggs, lightly beaten	4
½ cup	granulated sugar	125 mL
½ tsp	vanilla	2 mL
¼ tsp	salt	1 mL
Pinch	almond extract	Pinch
	Ground nutmeg	

- *Preheat oven to 400°F (200°C)*
- *Baking sheet*

1. Chill pie shell in refrigerator while preparing recipe.
2. In a medium saucepan, scald milk (see tip, page 86). Remove from heat.
3. In a large bowl, whisk eggs, sugar, vanilla, salt and almond extract. Gradually stir in scalded milk. Pour into chilled pie shell and sprinkle nutmeg over top. Place pie shell on baking sheet.
4. Bake in preheated oven for 25 to 30 minutes, or until custard is set and a knife inserted near the center comes out clean. Cool on wire rack, then chill in refrigerator for 3 to 4 hours or overnight.

Rhubarb Meringue Custard

SERVES 8 TO 12

½ cup	butter or margarine, softened	125 mL
2¼ cups	all-purpose flour, divided	550 mL
2 tbsp + 2 cups	granulated sugar	25 mL + 500 mL
6	egg yolks	6
1 cup	whipping (35%) cream	250 mL
¼ tsp	salt	1 mL
5 cups	chopped fresh rhubarb (about 1½ lbs/750 g)	1.25 L
Meringue		
6	egg whites	6
1 tsp	vanilla	5 mL
¼ tsp	salt	1 mL
¾ cup	granulated sugar	175 mL

TIP: For the best volume, bring egg whites to room temperature before beating. If you have forgotten to remove eggs from the refrigerator to allow them to come to room temperature, place them in a bowl of warm water for several minutes.

- *Preheat oven to 350°F (180°C)*
- *13- by 9-inch (3 L) baking dish, ungreased*

1. In a small mixer bowl, on low speed, beat butter, 2 cups (500 mL) of the flour and the 2 tbsp (25 mL) sugar for about 2 minutes, scraping sides of bowl often, until mixture resembles coarse crumbs. Press into bottom of prepared baking dish and bake in preheated oven for 15 minutes. Raise oven temperature to 400°F (200°C).

2. In a large mixer bowl, on medium speed, beat egg yolks well. Add the 2 cups (500 mL) of sugar, whipping cream, the remaining ¼ cup (50 mL) of flour and salt and beat for 2 minutes, until smooth. Stir in rhubarb, mixing well. Pour over hot baked crust and bake for 45 to 55 minutes, or until filling is firm to the touch.

3. *Prepare meringue:* In a clean small mixer bowl, on high speed, beat egg whites for 2 minutes, or until soft peaks form. Add vanilla and salt; continue beating and gradually add sugar, beating until stiff peaks form. Spread over hot filling and seal around the edges.

4. Bake for another 6 to 8 minutes, or until meringue is lightly browned. Cool completely on wire rack before serving.

Microwave Egg Custard

SERVES 4

3	eggs	3
½ cup	granulated sugar	125 mL
1 tsp	vanilla	5 mL
Pinch	salt	Pinch
1½ cups	milk	375 mL
	Ground nutmeg or cinnamon	

1. Whisk eggs in a 4-cup (1 L) microwave-safe dish. Add sugar, vanilla and salt and whisk until well blended.

2. In a small microwave-safe dish, scald milk on High for 2 to 3 minutes. Slowly stir into egg mixture. Cover with plastic wrap and microwave on Low for about 10 minutes. Remove cover and sprinkle on nutmeg or cinnamon, or both.

Grandma's Egg Custard

SERVES 6 TO 8

2 cups	whole milk or light (5%) cream	500 mL
5	egg yolks	5
1/4 cup	granulated sugar	50 mL
1 tsp	vanilla	5 mL

TIP: When cooling custards in the refrigerator, put a piece of plastic wrap over top to prevent a skin from forming.

VARIATION: Spoon custard over fresh fruit, or place dessert glasses in refrigerator to chill and serve cold.

- *Double boiler*

1. In a heavy saucepan, scald milk (see tip, page 86). Remove from heat.
2. In a large mixer bowl, on low speed, beat egg yolks and sugar until blended. Gradually beat in hot milk and pour mixture into top of double boiler over simmering, not boiling, water. Cook, stirring constantly, for about 10 to 12 minutes, or until the mixture thickens enough to coat the back of a metal spoon. Remove from heat and stir in vanilla.
3. Spoon into individual dessert or parfait glasses, filling each about three-quarters full, and serve.

Old-Time Vanilla Custards

SERVES 4

2	eggs, lightly beaten	2
2 cups	milk	500 mL
1/3 cup + 1 tbsp	packed brown sugar	90 mL
1 1/2 tsp	vanilla	7 mL
Pinch	salt (optional)	Pinch
	Ground nutmeg	

- *Preheat oven to 350°F (180°C)*
- *Four 3/4-cup (175 mL) custard cups or ramekins*
- *13- by 9-inch (3 L) baking pan*

1. In a small mixer bowl, combine eggs, milk, brown sugar, vanilla and salt, if using. Beat on medium speed until well blended. Spoon into custard cups and sprinkle with nutmeg.
2. Place cups in baking pan set on oven rack and pour in hot water until it reaches halfway up the cups. Bake in preheated oven for 30 to 35 minutes, or until custard is set and a knife inserted near the center comes out clean. Remove cups to wire rack to cool. Serve warm or chilled.

Rice Custard and Fruit

SERVES 6

2 cups	milk	500 mL
4	egg yolks	4
¼ cup	granulated sugar	50 mL
Pinch	salt	Pinch
1 to 1½ cups	cooked white rice	250 to 375 mL
½ tsp	vanilla	2 mL
	Sliced almonds, toasted	
1	package (10 oz/300 g) frozen fruit (such as strawberries or raspberries), thawed	1

- *Double boiler*
- *Six ¾-cup (175 mL) custard cups or ramekins*

1. In a medium saucepan, scald milk (see tip, page 86). Remove from heat.
2. In top of double boiler, over simmering but not boiling water, whisk egg yolks, sugar and salt. Gradually beat in scalded milk and stir until mixture thickens enough to coat the back of a metal spoon, about 10 minutes. Stir in rice and vanilla.
3. Spoon into custard cups and top with almonds. Serve warm or chilled, topped with fruit.

Sweet Potato Custard

SERVES 8

½ cup	golden raisins	125 mL
1 tbsp	brandy extract or brandy	15 mL
1½ lbs	sweet potatoes, peeled and sliced (about 3 cups/750 mL)	750 g
4	small eggs, beaten	4
1 cup	milk	250 mL
½ cup	evaporated milk	125 mL
1½ tbsp	granulated sugar	22 mL
1 tsp	ground cinnamon	5 mL
¼ tsp	ground nutmeg	1 mL
¼ tsp	ground mace	1 mL

- *Preheat oven to 350°F (180°C)*
- *12-cup (3 L) casserole dish, ungreased*
- *13- by 9-inch (3 L) baking pan*

1. In a small bowl, combine raisins, 2 tbsp (25 mL) hot water and brandy. Mix well and set aside.
2. Overlap potato slices in the bottom of casserole dish. Drain the raisin mixture, reserving the liquid, and sprinkle raisins over potato slices.
3. In a medium bowl, combine the reserved raisin liquid, eggs, milk, evaporated milk, sugar, cinnamon, nutmeg and mace. Mix together until well blended and pour evenly over the potato slices and raisins.
4. Place casserole dish into baking pan set on oven rack and pour in hot water until it reaches halfway up the dish. Bake in preheated oven for 50 to 60 minutes, or until a knife inserted near the center comes out clean and the custard is set. Remove casserole dish from pan of water and cool on wire rack. Serve warm.

Vegetable Cheese Custard

SERVES 6 TO 8

2	packages (each 10 oz/300 g) frozen mixed vegetables	2
2 cups	milk	500 mL
1 tbsp	grated onion	15 mL
1 tsp	parsley flakes	5 mL
½ tsp	salt	2 mL
4	eggs, lightly beaten	4
1	package (8 oz/250 g) processed American (or other) cheese, shredded	1

- *Preheat oven to 350°F (180°C)*
- *6-cup (1.5 L) casserole dish, ungreased*
- *13- by 9-inch (3 L) baking pan*

1. In a large saucepan, cook vegetables according to instructions on package. Drain and spoon into casserole dish.

2. In a medium saucepan, combine milk, onion, parsley and salt and cook until milk is scalded (see tip, page 86). Slowly stir in eggs.

3. Sprinkle shredded cheese over vegetables and pour egg mixture over top.

4. Place casserole dish in baking pan and pour in boiling water until it reaches halfway up the dish. Bake in preheated oven for 45 to 50 minutes, or until custard is set and a knife inserted near the center comes out clean. Remove casserole dish from pan of water and cool on wire rack. Serve warm.

Pepper Corn Custard

SERVES 4 TO 6

4	eggs	4
¾ cup	sour cream	175 mL
½ cup	shredded old Cheddar cheese (about 2 oz/60 g)	125 mL
½ tsp	salt	2 mL
Pinch	ground black pepper	Pinch
½	sweet red pepper, chopped	½
2½ cups	corn kernels (about 3 cobs)	625 mL

- *Preheat oven to 350°F (180°C)*
- *6-cup (1.5 L) casserole dish, greased*

1. In a medium bowl, whisk eggs until well beaten. Add sour cream, cheese, salt and black pepper, whisking until well incorporated.

2. Sprinkle red pepper and corn into prepared casserole dish. Spoon egg mixture over top.

3. Bake in preheated oven for 1 hour, or until slightly puffed and top is golden brown. Cool slightly on a wire rack and serve with a salad, or as desired.

Crème Brûlée

SERVES 6

2 cups	whipping (35%) cream	500 mL
4	egg yolks	4
¼ cup	granulated sugar	50 mL
½ tsp	vanilla	2 mL
3 tbsp	brown sugar	45 mL
	Fresh seasonal fruit	

- *Six ½-cup (125 mL) custard cups or ramekins*
- *Jelly-roll pan or rimmed baking sheet*

1. In a medium saucepan, heat cream over medium heat to scalding (until tiny bubbles form around the edges).

2. In a heavy medium saucepan, combine egg yolks and sugar and whisk until well blended. Gradually stir in scalded cream and cook, stirring, over medium-low heat, until mixture has thickened enough to coat the back of a metal spoon, about 12 to 15 minutes. Do not boil. Stir in vanilla.

3. Pour mixture into custard cups, dividing equally. Place in refrigerator for 3 to 4 hours, or until well chilled. An hour or two before ready to serve, preheat the broiler.

4. Put the brown sugar in a small strainer and press with the back of a spoon so that it comes through the sieve and over the creamed mixture in the cups.

5. Place the cups on the jelly-roll pan and set under broiler for 2 to 3 minutes, just until sugar melts. Return to refrigerator and chill for 1 to 2 hours, or until the melted sugar forms a crisp crust over the custard. (If you do this too long before serving, the sugar will lose its crispness.)

6. To serve, place each cup on a serving plate. Cut fresh seasonal fruit into slices or chunks and spoon over top.

Individual Caramel Flans

SERVES 4

⅔ cup	granulated sugar, divided	150 mL
3	eggs	3
1½ cups	milk	375 mL
1 tsp	vanilla	5 mL
	Ground cinnamon or nutmeg (optional)	

VARIATION: Substitute an equal amount of brown sugar for the second ⅓ cup (75 mL) of granulated sugar.

- *Preheat oven to 325°F (160°C)*
- *Four ¾-cup (175 mL) custard cups or ramekins*
- *9-inch (2.5 L) square baking dish*

1. In a heavy skillet, over medium-high heat, cook ⅓ cup (75 mL) of the sugar to caramelize. Do not stir, but shake pan a few times to heat evenly. When sugar begins to melt, reduce heat to low and cook, stirring as needed, until all of the sugar is melted and golden, about 5 minutes. Divide the mixture equally among the custard cups, tilting the cups to coat the bottoms evenly. Set aside for 10 minutes.

2. Meanwhile, in a small mixer bowl, on medium speed, beat eggs, milk, the other ⅓ cup (75 mL) sugar and vanilla until well blended but not foamy. Spoon into custard cups, dividing equally. Sprinkle some cinnamon or nutmeg, or both, over top.

3. Place cups in baking dish set on oven rack and pour in boiling water until it reaches halfway up the cups. Bake in preheated oven for 30 to 45 minutes, or until custard is set and a knife inserted near the center comes out clean. Remove cups to wire rack to cool completely. Cover tightly with plastic wrap and chill in refrigerator for 3 to 4 hours or overnight.

4. When ready to serve, loosen edges with a knife, invert a serving plate over the top of each cup, then flip cup and plate. Remove the cups to leave individual caramel flans on the serving plates.

Pumpkin Loaf Flan

SERVES 8 TO 10

1 ⅓ cup	granulated sugar, divided	325 mL
6	eggs	6
2 cups	canned pumpkin purée	500 mL
2 cups	whipping (35%) cream	500 mL
1 tsp	ground cinnamon	5 mL
½ tsp	salt	2 mL
½ tsp	ground ginger	2 mL
¼ tsp	ground allspice	1 mL
	Whipped topping (optional)	

- *Preheat oven to 350°F (180°C)*
- *9- by 5-inch (2 L) glass loaf pan, ungreased*
- *13- by 9-inch (3 L) baking pan*

1. In a heavy skillet, combine ⅔ cup (150 mL) of the sugar and ¼ cup (50 mL) water and bring to a boil, stirring until sugar is dissolved. Cook syrup, swirling pan but not stirring, until mixture is a deep caramel. Pour into loaf pan and tilt pan to coat the bottom evenly. Set aside to harden.

2. In a large mixer bowl, on medium speed, beat eggs, pumpkin, whipping cream, the other ⅔ cup (150 mL) sugar, cinnamon, salt, ginger and allspice, beating until mixture is well combined. Pour into loaf pan evenly.

3. Place in baking pan set on oven rack and pour in hot water until it reaches halfway up the sides of the loaf pan. Bake in preheated oven for 75 minutes, or until a knife inserted near the center comes out clean. Remove loaf pan to wire rack to cool. Cover tightly with plastic wrap and chill overnight.

4. When ready to serve, run a knife around the edge of loaf pan, invert a platter over the pan, then flip over the platter and pan. Remove the loaf pan. Cut into slices to serve, topped with whipped topping, if desired.

Mousses

Creamy Apricot Mousse

SERVES 6 TO 8

1 cup	dried apricots (about 8 oz/250 g)	250 mL
1	envelope ($\frac{1}{4}$ oz/7 g) unflavored gelatin powder	1
2	egg yolks	2
$\frac{3}{4}$ cup	granulated sugar	175 mL
2 tbsp	freshly squeezed orange juice	25 mL
2 cups	whipping (35%) cream	500 mL
	Fresh apricots, halved, for garnish	

VARIATION: Substitute an equal amount of orange liqueur for the orange juice.

- *Double boiler*

1. Place the apricots in a small saucepan and add enough water just to cover by about 1 inch (2.5 cm). Set aside for 30 minutes.
2. In a small bowl, combine 2 tbsp (25 mL) cold water and gelatin to soften.
3. Place saucepan with apricots over medium-high heat and heat to boiling. Reduce heat and simmer, uncovered, for about 25 minutes, or until apricots become tender.
4. Place hot apricots and water in a food processor with the softened gelatin and process until smooth. Let stand to cool to room temperature.
5. In another small bowl, whisk egg yolks, sugar and orange juice until well mixed. Transfer mixture to the top of double boiler, over simmering water, and whisk until mixture is hot to the touch and slightly thickened. Do not overcook. Set aside and whisk until slightly cool.
6. In a small mixer bowl, beat whipping cream until stiff peaks form.
7. In a large bowl, mix together the cooled egg mixture and apricot mixture and fold in the whipped cream. Spoon into individual dessert dishes or glasses. Garnish with a fresh apricot half, or as desired.

Choco-Raspberry Mousse Dessert

SERVES 6 TO 8

3	squares (each 1 oz/30 g) unsweetened baking chocolate	3
½ cup	butter or margarine, softened	125 mL
3	eggs, lightly beaten	3
1 cup	granulated sugar	250 mL
1 tsp	vanilla	5 mL
⅔ cup	all-purpose flour	150 mL
½ tsp	baking powder	2 mL
Pinch	salt	Pinch

Mousse Topping

1	package (10 oz/300 g) frozen raspberries in syrup, thawed	1
1	envelope (¼ oz/7 g) unflavored gelatin powder	1
½ cup	granulated sugar	125 mL
2 tbsp	freshly squeezed lemon juice	25 mL
1¼ cups	whipping (35%) cream	300 mL

TIPS: For a change, use frozen strawberries in syrup, or any other frozen berries, in place of the raspberries.

If desired, whip an additional ¾ cup (175 mL) whipping cream and use to decorate the top of the dessert.

- *Preheat oven to 350°F (180°C)*
- *9-inch (2.5 L) square baking dish, greased*

1. In a medium saucepan, over low heat, combine chocolate and butter and stir constantly until melted and smooth. Remove from heat and stir in eggs, sugar and vanilla, stirring until well blended.

2. In a medium bowl, mix together flour, baking powder and salt until combined. Pour in chocolate mixture and mix well. Spoon into prepared baking dish, spreading evenly, and bake at 350°F (180°C) for 25 to 30 minutes, or until set. Set aside to cool.

3. *Prepare mousse topping:* Drain raspberries, reserving the syrup. Cut the raspberries into halves or pieces. Add water to the reserved syrup to make 1¼ cups (300 mL) of liquid.

4. In a medium saucepan, combine gelatin and sugar. Add raspberry liquid and lemon juice and bring to a boil, stirring constantly until dissolved. Remove from heat and chill in refrigerator for 2 to 4 hours, or until mixture begins to set.

5. In a small mixer bowl, on high speed, beat whipping cream until stiff peaks form.

6. In a large bowl, whisk gelatin mixture well until light. Fold in whipped cream and then raspberries and spoon over chocolate base in baking dish. Chill in refrigerator for 1 to 2 hours, until set.

Divine Chocolate Mousse

SERVES 6

1 cup	granulated sugar, divided	250 mL
4	squares (each 1 oz/30 g) unsweetened baking chocolate, chopped	4
1 tbsp	strong brewed coffee	15 mL
3	egg whites (see tip, below)	3
½ cup	frozen whipped topping, thawed	125 mL
	Mint leaves	
	Berries	

TIP: This recipe contains raw egg whites. If the food safety of raw egg whites is a concern for you, substitute 6 tbsp (90 mL) pasteurized egg whites, found in the refrigerated egg section of most supermarkets. Alternatively, omit egg whites and increase whipped topping to 1½ cups (375 mL).

1. In a small saucepan, over low heat, combine ¾ cup (175 mL) of the sugar and ¼ cup (50 mL) water and stir until sugar is dissolved. Remove from heat and add the chocolate. Whisk until chocolate is completely melted and smooth. Add the coffee and whisk to blend. Pour mixture into a large bowl.
2. In a small mixer bowl, on high speed, beat egg whites until soft peaks form. Slowly add the remaining ¼ cup (50 mL) of sugar and continue beating until stiff, but not dry, peaks form. Fold about one-quarter of the beaten egg whites into the chocolate mixture. Then fold in the remaining beaten egg whites. Fold in whipped topping until well blended.
3. Spoon into 6 individual dessert dishes and cover each tightly with plastic wrap. Chill in refrigerator for 3 to 4 hours. Garnish with a dollop of whipped topping and mint leaves or berries, or as desired.

Easy Mocha Mousse

SERVES 4

6	squares (each 1 oz/30 g) semi-sweet baking chocolate	6
½ cup	strong coffee	125 mL
2 cups	whipping (35%) cream	500 mL
2 tbsp	confectioner's (icing) sugar, sifted	25 mL
Mocha Whipped Topping		
½ cup	whipping (35%) cream	125 mL
1 tbsp	confectioner's (icing) sugar, sifted	15 mL
1 tsp	instant coffee granules	5 mL
¼ tsp	vanilla	1 mL

- *Small bowl, chilled*

1. In a small saucepan, over low heat, combine chocolate and coffee, stirring until melted and smooth. Remove from heat and pour into chilled bowl for faster cooling.
2. In a small mixer bowl, on high speed, beat cream, slowly adding the confectioner's sugar and beating until soft peaks form. Fold into chocolate mixture. Spoon into 4 individual dessert dishes and chill in refrigerator for 3 to 4 hours or overnight.
3. *Prepare mocha whipped topping:* In a small mixer bowl, combine whipping cream, confectioner's sugar, coffee granules and vanilla and beat, on high speed, until firm peaks form. Spoon over chilled mousse to garnish.

White Chocolate Mousse

SERVES 4

3	squares (each 1 oz/30 g) white baking chocolate	3
2	egg yolks	2
½	package (3 oz/85 g) unflavored gelatin powder	½
1 cup	whipping (35%) cream, whipped	250 mL

TIP: Garnish with your favorite sauce (see Sauces, pages 176–79), or with seasonal fruit.

- *Double boiler*

1. Melt chocolate in double boiler, over low heat, stirring until smooth and creamy.
2. In a small mixer bowl, on medium speed, beat egg yolks until light and fluffy. Add melted chocolate until blended.
3. In a small bowl, dissolve the gelatin in 6 tbsp (90 mL) hot water. Pour into chocolate mixture and whisk gently until blended. Chill in refrigerator for 2 to 4 hours, or until mixture mounds slightly.
4. Fold whipped cream into chocolate mixture, whisking just until blended. Spoon into 4 individual dessert dishes and chill in refrigerator for 3 to 4 hours, or overnight.

Kahlúa Chocolate Mousse

SERVES 4

3	squares (each 1 oz/30 g) semi-sweet baking chocolate	3
¼ cup	butter or margarine	50 mL
¼ cup	Kahlúa liqueur, divided	50 mL
2	egg yolks	2
1 ½ tsp	granulated sugar	7 mL
1 cup	whipping (35%) cream	250 mL

- *Double boiler*

1. In a small saucepan, over low heat, melt chocolate and butter. Stir in 2 tbsp (25 mL) of the Kahlúa and mix to blend. Set aside.
2. In the top of a double boiler, whisk egg yolks and the remaining 2 tbsp (25 mL) of Kahlúa. Add sugar and whisk until slightly thickened and color lightens. Place over boiling water and stir until thickened, about 10 to 12 minutes. Remove top of double boiler and set in a large bowl or pan of cold water. Beat until mixture is thick, about 3 to 5 minutes. Add chocolate mixture to egg mixture and mix together until well blended.
3. In a small mixer bowl, beat whipping cream until stiff peaks form. Fold into the chocolate mixture. Spoon into 4 individual dessert dishes or glasses and chill in refrigerator for 3 to 4 hours, or until ready to serve. Garnish as desired.

Lemon Mousse with Fresh Berries

SERVES 8

2	eggs	2
6	egg yolks	6
1 cup	granulated sugar	250 mL
1 1/2 tbsp	grated lemon zest	22 mL
3/4 cup	freshly squeezed lemon juice	175 mL
2 cups	whipping (35%) cream, divided	500 mL
	Assorted berries, tossed with granulated sugar	

● *Double boiler*

1. In a double boiler, over simmering water, combine eggs, egg yolks, sugar, lemon zest and lemon juice. Mix well. Whisk until mixture thickens, then transfer to a large bowl. Chill in refrigerator, whisking occasionally, until cool.

2. In a small mixer bowl, on high speed, beat 1 1/2 cups (375 mL) of the whipping cream until firm peaks form. Fold one-third of the whipped cream into the lemon mixture just to lighten, then fold in the remaining whipped cream.

3. Spoon berry-sugar mixture into 8 individual dessert dishes, dividing equally. Spoon lemon mixture over top.

4. In the small mixer bowl, on high speed, beat the remaining 1/2 cup (125 mL) whipping cream until stiff peaks form. Spoon over each dish.

Refreshing Lemon-Lime Mousse

SERVES 6

1/2 cup	granulated sugar	125 mL
2 tbsp	cornstarch	25 mL
Pinch	salt	Pinch
3	egg yolks	3
2/3 cup	milk	150 mL
1 1/2 tsp	grated lemon zest	7 mL
1/4 cup	freshly squeezed lemon juice	50 mL
1/2 tsp	grated lime zest	2 mL
1 tbsp	freshly squeezed lime juice	15 mL
1 cup	whipping (35%) cream	250 mL
	Lemon or lime slices	
	Additional grated lemon or lime zest, for garnish (optional)	

1. In a medium saucepan, mix together sugar, cornstarch and salt.

2. In a small bowl, whisk together egg yolks and milk and add to the sugar mixture. Add lemon and lime juices and whisk until blended and smooth. Cook over medium heat, stirring until mixture comes to a boil. Then cook and stir for 2 minutes longer. Stir in the grated lemon and lime zests and cover tightly with plastic wrap. Chill in refrigerator until completely cooled.

3. In a small mixer bowl, whip cream until firm peaks form. Fold into cooled mixture. Spoon into 6 individual dessert dishes and garnish with lemon or lime slices and zests, if desired.

Quick 'n' Easy Orange Mousse

SERVES 6

1	can (10 oz/284 g) mandarin orange segments	1
1	package (3 oz/85 g) orange gelatin powder	1
1 cup	boiling water	250 mL
1	can (6 oz/160 mL) evaporated milk, chilled	1

- *4-cup (1 L) glass dessert bowl*

1. Drain the mandarin orange segments, reserving liquid. Add enough water to the liquid to bring it to 1 cup (250 mL).

2. In a medium bowl, dissolve gelatin in boiling water, stirring until completely dissolved. Add the reserved orange liquid and mix well. Cool in refrigerator until slightly thickened.

3. In another medium bowl, whisk chilled milk, then beat with an electric beater until thick. Stir in slightly thickened gelatin and whisk to blend.

4. Arrange some of the mandarin orange segments in bottom of dessert bowl. Spoon gelatin mixture over top. Garnish with remaining orange segments. Chill in refrigerator until ready to serve.

Pineapple Nut Mousse

SERVES 6

1	package (3 oz/85 g) pineapple or lemon gelatin powder	1
1 cup	canned crushed pineapple, with liquid	250 mL
Pinch	salt (optional)	Pinch
1 cup	whipping (35%) cream, whipped	250 mL
1/4 cup	chopped nuts (pecans or other)	50 mL

1. In a medium saucepan, bring 1 cup (250 mL) water to a boil. Stir in gelatin until completely dissolved. Add crushed pineapple and salt, if using, and mix together. Spoon into a medium bowl and chill in refrigerator until slightly thickened.

2. Gently fold in whipped cream and nuts until well combined. Spoon into 6 individual dessert dishes, dividing equally, and chill in refrigerator until firm. Garnish as desired.

Pumpkin Pie Mousse

SERVES 6

1	envelope (¼ oz/7 g) unflavored gelatin powder	1
¾ cup	firmly packed brown sugar	175 mL
1½ tsp	ground cinnamon	7 mL
¼ tsp	ground nutmeg	1 mL
¼ tsp	ground ginger	1 mL
1½ cups	canned pumpkin purée	375 mL
1 cup	evaporated milk	250 mL
3	egg whites (see tip, below)	3
Pinch	salt	Pinch
	Grated lemon zest (optional)	

TIP: This recipe contains raw egg whites. If the food safety of raw egg whites is a concern for you, substitute 6 tbsp (90 mL) pasteurized egg whites, found in the refrigerated egg section of most supermarkets. Alternatively, omit egg whites and use 1 cup (250 mL) frozen whipped topping, thawed.

1. In a medium saucepan, over medium heat, combine gelatin, brown sugar, cinnamon, nutmeg and ginger. Mix together. Stir in pumpkin and milk and cook for about 10 minutes, stirring constantly, until gelatin is completely dissolved. Spoon into a large bowl and set aside to cool until mixture mounds when dropped from a spoon.

2. In a small mixer bowl, on medium speed, beat egg whites and salt until stiff peaks form. Fold into pumpkin mixture, mixing until well combined. Spoon into 6 individual dessert dishes. Cover tightly with plastic wrap and chill in refrigerator for 3 to 4 hours or overnight. Garnish with grated zest, if desired.

Frozen Strawberry Mousse

SERVES 4 TO 6

1	package (10 oz/300 g) frozen sweetened strawberries	1
½ cup	granulated sugar	125 mL
½ cup	sour cream	125 mL
1 tsp	vanilla	5 mL
	Fresh strawberries	

- *9-inch (2.5 L) square baking dish*

1. In a food processor or blender, combine strawberries, sugar, sour cream and vanilla and process until blended and smooth. Spoon into baking dish, cover tightly with plastic wrap and place in the freezer until frozen.

2. When ready to serve, spoon into 4 to 6 individual dessert dishes. Garnish with fresh strawberries, whole or sliced.

Puddings

continued on next page

When you are making pudding that calls for either sugar and flour or sugar and cornstarch, it is best to mix the sugar with the flour or cornstarch before mixing them with the other ingredients. This method will always produce a smooth pudding.

Phyllo Cups

MAKES 12 PHYLLO CUPS

3	sheets phyllo pastry	3
¼ cup	butter, melted	50 mL
2 tbsp	granulated sugar	25 mL

TIP: Rather than use custard cups or dessert dishes, a fancy, decorative way to serve puddings is to bake phyllo cups, spoon the pudding into the cup and then top with fruit, whipped topping or any other desired garnish.

- *Preheat oven to 375°F (190°C)*
- *12-cup muffin tin, ungreased*

1. Place 1 sheet of phyllo on a flat work surface. Cover the remaining sheets with a damp towel to prevent them from drying out.

2. Brush the phyllo sheet generously with one-third of the melted butter. Lay a second sheet over top and brush with another third of the butter. Place the third sheet on top and, with a rolling pin, press the three layers firmly together, forming a rectangle. Brush the top with the remaining butter and sprinkle sugar over top.

3. Cut rectangle in half lengthwise, then cut each half into 3 equal rectangles and press into the cups of the muffin tin.

4. Bake in preheated oven for 7 to 10 minutes, or until crisp and golden brown. Cool on wire rack. When ready to serve, fill with prepared pudding and garnish as desired.

Old-Fashioned Cottage Pudding

SERVES 6 TO 8

1 cup	granulated sugar	250 mL
¼ cup	shortening	50 mL
1	egg	1
¼ tsp	lemon extract	1 mL
1¾ cups	sifted all-purpose flour	425 mL
2½ tsp	baking powder	12 mL
½ tsp	salt	2 mL
⅔ cup	milk	150 mL

TIP: This pudding tastes great with a lemon sauce, such as the one on page 141.

- *Preheat oven to 350°F (180°C)*
- *8-inch (2 L) square baking dish, buttered*

1. In a large mixer bowl, cream sugar and shortening until smooth. Add egg and lemon extract and beat well.
2. In a medium bowl, sift together flour, baking powder and salt. Add to creamed mixture alternately with the milk, beating after each addition. Spoon into prepared baking dish.
3. Bake in preheated oven for 30 to 35 minutes, or until pudding is set and top is golden brown. Cool slightly on a wire rack and serve warm.

Quick Pudding Cake

SERVES 12 TO 16

1	package (18 oz/510 g) double-layer cake mix	1
2	packages (each 4 oz/113 g) instant pudding mix	2
1 cup	confectioner's (icing) sugar, sifted	250 mL
4 cups	cold milk	1 L

TIP: This recipe is a quick, easy way to make a plain cake into a moist, delicious pudding cake. It's great because you can use any plain homemade cake, or any flavor cake mix, and any flavor pudding mix.

- *13- by 9-inch (3 L) baking pan*

1. Prepare cake mix as directed on the package (or prepare a homemade cake as per your recipe). As soon as cake is removed from oven, poke holes down through the cake to the pan using a plastic drinking straw or the round handle of a wooden spoon. Use a gentle turning motion to make large enough holes. Set cake aside.
2. In a large mixer bowl, mix together pudding mix and sugar. Slowly add the milk and stir to combine. Beat for 1 minute, on low speed, and immediately pour one-half of the thin pudding evenly over the top of warm cake so that it falls into the holes to make the stripes.
3. Let the remaining pudding thicken slightly, then spoon over the cake, using a swirling motion as you would when frosting a cake. Chill in refrigerator for at least 1 hour or until ready to serve.

Last-Minute Pudding Loaf Cake

SERVES 10 TO 12

1	package (18 oz/510 g) cake mix	1
1	package (4 oz/113 g) instant pudding mix	1
4	eggs, lightly beaten	4
1/3 cup	vegetable oil	75 mL

TIP: Here's another quick recipe that can be made with any flavor cake mix and pudding mix.

- *Preheat oven to 350°F (180°C)*
- *9- by 5-inch (2 L) loaf pan, greased*

1. In a large mixer bowl, mix cake mix and pudding mix together. Make a well in the center. Add eggs, 1 cup (250 mL) cold water and oil and beat on low speed, just until moist, blended and smooth. Pour into prepared baking pan.
2. Bake in preheated oven for 50 to 55 minutes, or until a toothpick inserted in the center of cake comes out clean and dry. Cool on wire rack.

English Bakewell Pudding

SERVES 6 TO 8

8 oz	puff pastry, thawed if frozen (a little more than half a package)	250 g
1 cup	strawberry jam	250 mL
1/3 cup + 2 tbsp	sugar	100 mL
1/3 cup + 2 tbsp	butter	100 mL
4	egg yolks	4
2	egg whites, beaten	2
1/2 tsp	almond extract	2 mL

- *Preheat oven to 425°F (220°C)*
- *9-inch (23 cm) pie plate or wide, shallow dish, ungreased*

1. Roll out the puff pastry on a floured work surface. Line pie plate with the pastry. Spread a thick layer of jam over pastry, using whatever amount you desire.
2. In a medium bowl, cream the sugar and butter. Add egg yolks, egg whites and almond extract, beating just until well blended. Spread over jam.
3. Bake in preheated oven for 15 minutes, then reduce oven temperature to 350°F (180°C) and bake for an additional 20 minutes, until pudding is set and top is golden brown. Cool on wire rack.

Old-Fashioned Indian Pudding

SERVES 6 TO 8

½ cup	yellow cornmeal	125 mL
5 cups	milk, divided	1.25 L
½ cup	granulated sugar	125 mL
½ cup	fancy molasses	125 mL
¼ cup	butter or margarine	50 mL
1 tsp	salt	5 mL
1 tsp	pumpkin pie spice	5 mL

TIP: Best when served warm with ice cream.

VARIATION: Some of the original recipes use 1 tsp (5 mL) ground ginger instead of the pumpkin pie spice.

- *Preheat oven to 325°F (160°C)*
- *8-cup (2 L) casserole dish, buttered*

1. In a large, heavy saucepan, over medium-low heat, combine cornmeal, 2 cups (500 mL) of the milk, sugar, molasses, butter, salt and pumpkin pie spice. Stir to blend, heating slowly to boiling. Reduce heat to low and simmer for about 5 minutes, stirring constantly, until thick and creamy. Pour into prepared baking dish. Add another 2 cups (500 mL) of the milk and stir to blend well.

2. Bake in preheated oven for 1 hour. Remove from oven and stir in the remaining 1 cup (250 mL) milk. Bake for 2 hours longer, or until pudding sets.

Traditional Yorkshire Pudding

SERVES 12

1 cup	all-purpose flour	250 mL
½ tsp	salt	2 mL
2	eggs	2
1 cup	milk	250 mL
1 tsp	butter	5 mL

- *Preheat oven to 450°F (230°C)*
- *12-cup muffin tin, greased*

1. In a large mixer bowl, sift together flour and salt. Add eggs and beat well. Beat in about a third of the milk and butter, beating until batter is stiff. Allow to stand for a few minutes, then gradually add the remaining milk and beat until well blended.

2. Put muffin tin into oven to heat up for a few minutes. Remove from oven. Spoon batter into hot muffin cups and bake in preheated oven for 30 to 35 minutes, or until puffed and golden brown. Serve immediately.

Layered Pudding Squares

SERVES 12 TO 16

2 cups	all-purpose flour	500 mL
1 cup	cold butter or margarine	250 mL
1	package (8 oz/250 g) cream cheese, softened	1
1 cup	confectioner's (icing) sugar, sifted	250 mL
1 cup	frozen whipped topping, thawed	250 mL
2	packages (each 3½ oz/102 g) vanilla pudding mix	2
4	ripe bananas	4
2	packages (each 3 oz/85 g) strawberry gelatin powder	2

- *Preheat oven to 350°F (180°C)*
- *13- by 9-inch (3 L) baking pan, ungreased*

1. Place flour in a medium bowl and cut in the butter with a pastry blender or fork until mixture is crumbly. Set aside about ½ cup (125 mL) of this crumb mixture and press remaining mixture into baking pan. Bake in preheated oven for 18 to 20 minutes, or until golden brown. Set on wire rack to cool.

2. In a small mixer bowl, beat cream cheese and confectioner's sugar until smooth. Gently fold in the whipped topping. Spread evenly over cooled crust.

3. Prepare vanilla pudding mix according to package directions. Set aside to cool.

4. Slice 2 bananas and spread over cream cheese mixture. Spread cool vanilla pudding over bananas. Top with the reserved crumb mixture. Chill in refrigerator for 1 hour.

5. Prepare gelatin according to package directions. Chill in refrigerator for 30 minutes, or until partially set.

6. Pour gelatin over crumbs. Slice the remaining 2 bananas and spread over gelatin. Chill in refrigerator for at least 2 hours or until ready to serve. Cut into squares.

Frozen Butterscotch Dessert

SERVES 20 TO 24

1 gallon	vanilla ice cream, softened	3.8 L
1 cup	whipping (35%) cream	250 mL
1	package (3.5 oz/102 g) butterscotch pudding	1
	Chocolate chips	

1. In a large bowl, blend together ice cream and whipping cream. Add pudding and chocolate chips and mix in to blend well. Freeze for at least 3 hours or until ready to serve.

Apple Almond Pudding Cake

SERVES 6

4 cups	peeled, halved, cored and grated apples (about 4 medium)	1 L
1 cup	granulated sugar, divided	250 mL
2 cups	zwieback crumbs (about 12 biscuits)	500 mL
½ cup	whole blanched almonds, finely ground	125 mL
½ cup	butter or margarine, melted	125 mL

- *Preheat oven to 375°F (190°C)*
- *8-inch (2 L) square baking dish, buttered*

1. In a large bowl, toss together the apples and ½ cup (125 mL) of the sugar.
2. In another large bowl, mix the zwieback crumbs with the remaining ½ cup (125 mL) sugar. Add ground almonds and melted butter and mix to blend well.
3. In prepared baking dish, make layers of apple mixture and crumb mixture, starting and ending with apple mixture.
4. Bake in preheated oven for 45 to 50 minutes, or until golden brown and apples are tender. Serve warm.

Banana Cream Pudding

SERVES 6 TO 8

⅔ cup	firmly packed brown sugar	150 mL
⅓ cup	all-purpose flour	75 mL
2 cups	milk	500 mL
2	egg yolks, beaten	2
2 tbsp	butter or margarine	25 mL
1 tsp	vanilla	5 mL
1 cup	whipping (35%) cream, whipped	250 mL
6	ripe but firm bananas, sliced	6
⅓ cup	chopped nuts (optional)	75 mL

- *8-cup (2 L) glass bowl (as you would use for trifle)*

1. In a medium saucepan, over medium heat, mix together brown sugar and flour. Stir in milk and, stirring constantly, cook until bubbly and thickened. Continue cooking for 1 minute longer, then remove from heat.
2. Take a cupful (250 mL) of the hot mixture and stir into the beaten egg yolks; return this mixture to the saucepan. Bring to a boil and boil gently for 3 minutes, stirring constantly. Remove from heat. Add the butter and vanilla and stir until blended and smooth. Set aside to cool, stirring occasionally. When at room temperature, fold in the whipped cream.
3. Spoon about one-third of the pudding into the glass bowl. Spread half of the sliced bananas over top. Repeat the layers and top with the remaining pudding. Sprinkle the chopped nuts over top, if desired, or add a few extra slices of banana for decoration, or both. Cover tightly with plastic wrap and chill in refrigerator for at least 1 to hour or until ready to serve.

Apple-Raisin Pudding

SERVES 6 TO 8

1 cup	all-purpose flour	250 mL
1 tsp	ground cinnamon	5 mL
¾ tsp	baking soda	4 mL
¼ tsp	ground nutmeg	1 mL
Pinch	salt	Pinch
¾ cup	granulated sugar	175 mL
½ cup	shortening or butter, softened	125 mL
1	egg, lightly beaten	1
1 tsp	vanilla	5 mL
1½ cups	chopped apples (best with Spartan or McIntosh, about 2 small)	375 mL
1 cup	raisins	250 mL
1 tbsp	milk or table (18%) cream	15 mL

- *Preheat oven to 350°F (180°C)*
- *8-cup (2 L) casserole dish, greased*

1. In a medium bowl, combine flour, cinnamon, baking soda, nutmeg and salt, mixing well to blend.

2. In a large bowl, cream sugar and shortening until light and fluffy. Add egg and vanilla and blend well. Add flour mixture and stir just until blended.

3. Lightly fold in apples, raisins and milk just until well combined. Transfer to prepared casserole dish.

4. Bake, uncovered, in preheated oven for 50 to 60 minutes, or until golden brown. Serve warm your favorite sauce (see Sauces, pages 176–79), if desired.

Applesauce Noodle Pudding

SERVES 6 TO 8

¼ cup	shortening or butter	50 mL
8 oz	fine noodles, cooked and drained	250 g
3	eggs	3
½ cup	dry or fresh bread crumbs, divided	125 mL
¼ cup	granulated sugar	50 mL
1½ tsp	ground cinnamon	7 mL
3 cups	sweetened applesauce	750 mL

- *Preheat oven to 350°F (180°C)*
- *8-inch (2 L) square baking dish, greased*

1. In a skillet, melt shortening. Add the noodles and sauté until browned.

2. In a large mixer bowl, combine eggs, ¼ cup (50 mL) of the bread crumbs, sugar and cinnamon, beating until blended. Stir in noodles and mix well.

3. In the prepared baking dish, alternate layers of noodle mixture and applesauce, starting and ending with the noodles. Sprinkle the remaining bread crumbs over top.

4. Bake in preheated oven for 25 to 30 minutes, or until golden brown.

Layered Blueberry Crumb Pudding

SERVES 4 TO 6

1 cup	wafer crumbs (about 6 wafers, zwieback, graham wafer or other)	250 mL
¼ cup	granulated sugar	50 mL
½ tsp	ground cinnamon	2 mL
3 tbsp	butter or margarine	45 mL
2 cups	fresh or frozen, well-drained blueberries (about 12 oz/375 g)	500 mL
	Whipped topping or ice cream	

- *Preheat oven to 350°F (180°C)*
- *11- by 7-inch (2 L) baking dish, ungreased*

1. In a small bowl, mix together wafer crumbs, sugar and cinnamon until well blended. Cut in butter using a pastry blender or two knives until the mixture resembles coarse crumbs.

2. Spoon 1 cup (250 mL) of the blueberries into baking dish, top with half of the crumb mixture, then repeat layers.

3. Bake in preheated oven for 25 to 30 minutes, or until golden brown. Serve warm. Cut into squares and top with whipped topping or ice cream.

Butterscotch Pudding

SERVES 4 TO 6

¾ cup	packed brown sugar	175 mL
2 tbsp	butter or margarine	25 mL
2½ cups	cold milk, divided	625 mL
⅓ cup	cornstarch	75 mL
1	egg, beaten	1

TIP: Serve with whipped cream or any other topping.

- *Double boiler*

1. In the top of double boiler, over medium heat, combine brown sugar and butter and stir until caramelized and brown. Add 2 cups (500 mL) of the milk, stirring until dissolved.

2. In a small bowl, mix cornstarch with the remaining ½ cup (125 mL) milk and add to the brown sugar mixture. Stir until thickened. Add a little of this hot mixture to the beaten egg, then pour it into the pudding. Cook, stirring, for 2 minutes longer. Remove from heat.

3. Spoon into a glass serving bowl or individual dessert dishes and set aside to cool slightly. Cover tightly with plastic wrap so a film won't form on top of the pudding.

Favorite Pudding Cookies

MAKES 6 TO 7 DOZEN COOKIES

4 cups	all-purpose flour	1 L
1 tsp	baking soda	5 mL
1 tsp	cream of tartar	5 mL
1 cup	granulated sugar	250 mL
1 cup	confectioner's (icing) sugar, sifted	250 mL
1 cup	vegetable oil	250 mL
1 cup	butter or margarine, softened	250 mL
2	eggs	2
1	package (3.5 oz/102 g) instant pudding mix	1
1 tsp	vanilla	5 mL
	Additional granulated sugar	

- *Preheat oven to 350°F (180°C)*
- *Baking sheet, ungreased*

1. In a medium bowl, combine flour, baking soda and cream of tartar. Mix together.

2. In a large mixer bowl, cream sugar, confectioner's sugar, oil and butter until smooth. Beat in eggs, pudding and vanilla. Add flour mixture, mixing well to blend. Drop by tablespoonfuls (15 mL) onto baking sheet about 2 inches (5 cm) apart. Flatten each with the bottom of a glass dipped in sugar.

3. Bake in preheated oven for about 15 minutes, or until golden brown. Cool on wire rack.

TIPS: How many cookies you get depends on the size of your spoonfuls!

You can choose the flavor of instant pudding you prefer. My favorites are lemon and butterscotch.

Caramel Nut Pudding

SERVES 4 TO 6

2 cups	cold milk	500 mL
1 1/2 cups	packed brown sugar	375 mL
1 tbsp	butter or margarine	15 mL
3 tbsp	cornstarch	45 mL
1 tsp	vanilla	5 mL
1/2 cup	chopped walnuts	125 mL

1. In a small saucepan, over low heat, scald milk (see tip, page 86). Remove from heat.

2. In a large saucepan, over low heat, combine brown sugar and butter and stir well until melted and quite brown. Add the scalded milk and stir in the cornstarch. Remove from heat and whisk until well beaten. Add vanilla and stir in walnuts.

3. Spoon into individual dessert dishes or glasses and set aside to cool slightly.

TIP: Garnish with a dollop of whipped topping and sprinkle additional chopped nuts over top.

Cheese 'n' Raisins Pudding

SERVES 6 TO 8

12 oz	cottage cheese, drained	375 g
4 oz	cream cheese, softened	125 g
3	eggs, separated	3
1 cup	granulated sugar	250 mL
Pinch	salt	Pinch
3	egg yolks, hard-boiled and finely chopped	3
½ cup	raisins	125 mL
⅓ cup	butter or margarine, melted	75 mL
3 tbsp	all-purpose flour	45 mL
1 tsp	vanilla	5 mL

TIP: Don't beat egg whites in plastic bowls, as plastic retains oil. Use a very clean bowl with no traces of oil and very clean beaters.

- *Preheat oven to 325°F (160°C)*
- *6-cup (1.5 L) casserole dish, buttered*

1. Over a medium bowl, push the cottage cheese and cream cheese through a sieve. Set aside.
2. In a large mixer bowl, on medium speed, beat raw egg yolks. Add sugar and salt and beat until thick and light in color. Stir in boiled egg yolks, raisins, butter, flour, vanilla and the sieved cheese mixture. Mix together until well blended.
3. In a small mixer bowl, on high speed, beat egg whites until stiff but not dry. Fold gently into the egg-cheese mixture until thoroughly combined. Spoon into prepared casserole dish.
4. Bake in preheated oven for 30 to 35 minutes, or until firm and golden brown. Place on a wire rack to cool slightly.

Russian Cheese Pudding

SERVES 4 TO 6

4	egg yolks, hard-boiled	4
2 cups	dry cottage cheese (about 1 lb/500 g)	500 mL
3	eggs, separated	3
1 cup	granulated sugar	250 mL
¼ cup	butter, melted	50 mL
½ cup	raisins	125 mL
3 tbsp	all-purpose flour	45 mL
½ tsp	vanilla	2 mL
Pinch	salt	Pinch

- *Preheat oven to 300°F (150°C)*
- *6-cup (1.5 L) casserole dish, greased*

1. Over a medium bowl, put hard-boiled egg yolks and cheese through a fine sieve.
2. In a large bowl, whisk together raw egg yolks, sugar and butter, beating until well blended. Add the egg-cheese mixture and mix well. Stir in raisins, flour, vanilla and salt. Mix well until thoroughly blended.
3. In a small mixer bowl, beat egg whites until stiff peaks form. Fold into mixture gently. Spoon into prepared casserole dish.
4. Bake in preheated oven for 35 to 45 minutes, or until golden brown. Place on a wire rack to cool slightly.

Tart Red Cherry Pudding

SERVES 6 TO 8

1	egg, lightly beaten	1
1 cup	canned tart red cherries, with juice	250 mL
1/2 cup	coarsely chopped nuts	125 mL
1 tbsp	butter or margarine, melted	15 mL
1 cup	all-purpose flour	250 mL
1 cup	granulated sugar	250 mL
1 tsp	baking soda	5 mL
1/2 tsp	salt	2 mL

- *Preheat oven to 350°F (180°C)*
- *9-inch (2.5 L) square baking pan, greased*

1. In a medium bowl, combine egg, cherries, nuts and butter. Mix well.
2. In another medium bowl, mix together flour, sugar, baking soda and salt. Add to the cherry mixture, stirring until well blended. Spoon into prepared baking pan.
3. Bake in preheated oven for 35 to 40 minutes, or until lightly browned. Serve warm.

Divine Chocolate Pudding

SERVES 4

2/3 cup	unsweetened cocoa powder	150 mL
2 tbsp	cornstarch	25 mL
2 1/4 cups	milk, divided	550 mL
2	egg whites	2
1/2 cup	granulated sugar	125 mL
Pinch	salt	Pinch
1 tsp	vanilla	5 mL
4	strawberries	4
	Mint leaves for garnish	

1. In a large bowl, mix together cocoa and cornstarch until blended. Whisk in 3/4 cup (175 mL) of the milk until mixture is completely smooth.
2. In a small bowl, lightly whisk egg whites. Set aside.
3. In a large heavy saucepan, over high heat, whisk the remaining 1 1/2 cups (375 mL) milk, sugar and salt. Bring to a boil, whisking constantly, over high heat. Reduce heat to medium-high and add cocoa mixture. Bring to a boil, whisking constantly, for 3 minutes. Remove pan from heat and reduce heat to medium-low.
4. Whisk 1 cup (250 mL) of the hot cocoa mixture into the bowl of egg whites and then pour into the pan. Cook for 2 minutes, whisking constantly, but do not bring to a boil. Remove from heat. Add vanilla and mix until well blended and smooth.
5. Spoon into 4 individual dessert dishes and set aside to cool to room temperature. Cover tightly with plastic wrap and chill in refrigerator for 1 hour. When ready to serve, place a whole strawberry and a mint leaf on each.

Microwave Chocolate Pudding

SERVES 4

¾ cup	granulated sugar	175 mL
2 tbsp	cornstarch	25 mL
2 cups	milk	500 mL
2	squares (each 1 oz/30 g) unsweetened baking chocolate, chopped	2
½ tsp	vanilla	2 mL
Pinch	salt	Pinch

TIP: Garnish with whipped cream or fresh fruit, or as desired.

- *4-cup (1 L) microwave-safe bowl*
- *Four ¾-cup (175 mL) custard cups or ramekins*

1. In microwave-safe bowl, mix together sugar and cornstarch. Gradually stir in milk until well blended. Add the chopped chocolate and mix well.
2. Microwave, uncovered, on High for 5 minutes. Whisk thoroughly to blend in the chocolate. Microwave on High for 2 to 3 minutes, until boiling and thickened.
3. Stir in vanilla and salt. Spoon into custard cups and set aside to cool to room temperature.

Chocolate Puddin' Pie

SERVES 6 TO 8

1½ cups	chocolate wafer cookie crumbs (about 35 wafers)	375 mL
¼ cup	butter or margarine, melted	50 mL
⅔ cup	granulated sugar	150 mL
3½ tbsp	unsweetened cocoa powder	52 mL
3½ tbsp	cornstarch	52 mL
2 cups	milk	500 mL
⅓ cup	semi-sweet chocolate chips (about 2 oz/60 g)	75 mL
1½ tsp	vanilla	7 mL
	Whipped topping	

TIP: If you don't have a glass pie plate, any pie plate will do.

- *Preheat oven to 350°F (180°C)*
- *9-inch (23 cm) glass pie plate, ungreased*

1. In a small bowl, mix together cookie crumbs and butter until well blended. Set aside 2 to 3 tbsp (25 to 45 mL) of this crumb mixture for a topping, if desired, and press remaining mixture firmly into bottom and sides of pie plate. Bake in preheated oven for 10 minutes, then set aside to cool on wire rack.
2. In a medium saucepan, over medium heat, whisk sugar, cocoa and cornstarch. Slowly add the milk, whisking to combine. Stir constantly until mixture comes to a boil and thickens. Boil for 2 minutes, stirring constantly. Remove from heat. Add chocolate chips and vanilla and stir until chips have melted and mixture is smooth.
3. Spoon filling evenly into cooled pie crust. Cover tightly with plastic wrap to prevent a skin from forming over the top. Chill in refrigerator for at least 1 hour. When ready to serve, swirl whipped topping over top.

Chocolate Meringue Crumb Pudding

SERVES 6 TO 8

½ cup	fresh bread crumbs (about 1 slice)	250 mL
½ cup	fresh cake crumbs (see tip, below)	250 mL
2 cups	milk, divided	500 mL
1½	squares (each 1 oz/30 g) unsweetened baking chocolate, melted and cooled	1½
¾ cup	granulated sugar	175 mL
3	egg yolks	3
2 tbsp	butter or margarine, melted	25 mL
¼ tsp	salt	1 mL
½ tsp	vanilla	2 mL

Meringue Topping

3	egg whites	3
½ cup	confectioner's (icing) sugar, sifted	125 mL

TIP: To make your cake crumbs, you can use any kind of prepared cake you prefer.

- *Preheat oven to 325°F (160°C)*
- *Double boiler*
- *8-inch (2 L) square baking dish, greased*

1. In a small bowl, mix together bread crumbs and cake crumbs.

2. In the top of a double boiler, combine 1½ cups (375 mL) of the milk and crumbs. Stir in melted chocolate and sugar. Cook over boiling water until the mixture forms a smooth paste.

3. In a small bowl, whisk egg yolks and the remaining ½ cup (125 mL) milk. Add butter and salt and whisk until thickened. Stir egg mixture into the hot mixture and cook, stirring constantly, over medium-low heat, until mixture is thickened. Remove from heat. Add vanilla and stir to blend. Spoon mixture into prepared baking dish.

4. Bake in preheated oven for 25 to 30 minutes, or until set. Set aside to cool on wire rack. Raise oven temperature to 425°F (220°C).

5. *Prepare meringue topping:* In a small mixer bowl, on medium speed, beat egg whites to form soft peaks. Slowly add the confectioner's sugar and beat, on high speed, until stiff peaks form.

6. When the pudding has cooled slightly, spread the meringue evenly over top. Bake at 425°F (220°C) for about 5 to 6 minutes, or until meringue is golden brown. Chill for 3 to 4 hours or overnight.

Graham Wafer Chocolate Pudding

SERVES 8 TO 10

1½ cups	cornstarch	375 mL
1⅓ cups	granulated sugar	325 mL
⅓ cup + 1 tbsp	unsweetened cocoa powder	90 mL
Pinch	salt	Pinch
5½ cups	milk	1.375 L
1 tbsp	vanilla	15 mL
1 tbsp	butter or margarine (optional)	15 mL
30	Graham wafers (honey or chocolate), divided	30
	Whipped topping or ice cream	

- *8-inch (2 L) square glass baking dish, ungreased*

1. In a medium saucepan, combine cornstarch, sugar, cocoa and salt. Mix to blend. Stir in milk until smooth. Cook over medium heat to a rolling boil, stirring constantly. Boil for 1 minute, no more, and remove from heat. Stir in vanilla and butter, if using, until well combined and smooth.

2. Line baking pan with graham wafers. Spoon one-third of pudding mixture over top. Make two more layers of each wafers and pudding. Crumble remaining graham wafers over top. Serve warm with a dollop of whipped topping or ice cream.

Gingerbread Pudding with Peachy Sauce

SERVES 6 TO 8

1	package (14.5 oz/400 g) gingerbread cake mix	1
½ cup	prepared mincemeat	125 mL
Peach Sauce		
1	can (14 oz/398 mL) sliced peaches	1
¼ cup	granulated sugar	50 mL
1 tbsp	cornstarch	15 mL
¼ tsp	salt	1 mL
2 tbsp	butter or margarine	25 mL
¼ tsp	grated lemon zest	1 mL
1 tbsp	freshly squeezed lemon juice	15 mL
½ cup	prepared mincemeat	125 mL

- *Preheat oven to 350°F (180°C)*
- *8-inch (2 L) square baking dish, greased and lightly floured*

1. In a large mixer bowl, combine gingerbread mix and ¾ cup (175 mL) water, beating on medium speed for 2 to 3 minutes. Add mincemeat, beating until blended. Spoon into prepared baking dish.

2. Bake in preheated oven for 35 to 40 minutes, or until top is golden brown. Cool slightly on wire rack and cut into squares.

3. *Prepare peach sauce:* Drain the peaches, reserving the liquid. Add enough water to bring liquid to 1 cup (250 mL). In a medium saucepan, combine sugar, cornstarch and salt. Stir in the peach liquid and cook over medium heat, stirring constantly, until mixture becomes bubbly and thickened. Add butter, lemon zest and lemon juice. Stir in the peaches and mincemeat until well blended. Spoon over the warm gingerbread squares.

Coconut Meringue Pudding

SERVES 6 TO 8

1¼ cup	granulated sugar, divided	300 mL
¼ cup	cornstarch	50 mL
3 cups	milk	750 mL
4	eggs, separated	4
1 cup	flaked coconut	250 mL
1 tsp	vanilla	5 mL

- *Preheat oven to 350°F (180°C)*
- *8-inch (2 L) square baking dish, ungreased*

1. In a heavy saucepan, over medium heat, mix together ¾ cup (175 mL) of the sugar and cornstarch. Add milk and cook, stirring, until mixture becomes bubbly and thick. Cook for another 2 minutes, then remove from heat.

2. In a small bowl, whisk egg yolks. Stir in 1 cup (250 mL) of the hot milk mixture, then pour into saucepan. Cook and stir until mixture is boiling gently, then continue cooking and stirring for 2 minutes more. Remove pan from heat and set aside to cool to lukewarm. Add coconut and vanilla and stir until blended. Spoon into prepared baking dish.

3. In a small mixer bowl, beat egg whites until soft peaks form. Gradually add the remaining ½ cup (125 mL) of sugar and beat, on high speed, until stiff peaks form. Spread evenly over pudding, right to the edges so that pudding is sealed in.

4. Bake in preheated oven for 10 to 15 minutes, or until set and top is golden brown. Best when served at room temperature.

Date Nut Pudding

SERVES 4 TO 6

2	eggs	2
¾ cup	granulated sugar	175 mL
2 tbsp	all-purpose flour	25 mL
1 tsp	baking powder	5 mL
1 cup	chopped dates (about 6 oz/175 g)	250 mL
1 cup	chopped walnuts	250 mL
	Ground cinnamon	
	Vanilla ice cream or whipped topping	

- *Preheat oven to 300°F (150°C)*
- *6-cup (1.5 L) casserole dish, buttered*

1. In a large mixer bowl, on medium speed, beat eggs well. Gradually beat in sugar until mixture thickens.

2. In a medium bowl, sift together flour and baking powder. Add dates and walnuts and mix well to blend. Pour into egg mixture and mix on medium speed until well combined. Spoon into prepared baking pan and sprinkle cinnamon over top.

3. Bake in preheated oven for 30 to 35 minutes, or until set and top is golden brown. Cool on a wire rack and serve with vanilla ice cream or whipped topping (or any other desired topping).

Lemon Sponge Pudding

SERVES 4 TO 6

1 cup	granulated sugar	250 mL
3 tbsp	butter or margarine, softened	45 mL
⅓ cup	all-purpose flour	75 mL
3	eggs, separated	3
1 cup	milk	250 mL
1 tsp	lemon zest	5 mL
3 tbsp	freshly squeezed lemon juice	45 mL

- *Preheat oven to 325°F (160°C)*
- *8-cup (2 L) casserole dish, greased*

1. In a large bowl, cream sugar and butter until light and fluffy. Add flour and mix to blend.
2. In a small bowl, beat egg yolks well. Stir in milk, lemon zest and lemon juice, mixing until well blended. Pour into creamed mixture and mix well.
3. In a small mixer bowl, on high speed, beat egg whites until stiff peaks form. Gently fold into lemon mixture until well combined. Spoon into prepared casserole dish.
4. Bake in preheated oven for 50 to 60 minutes, or until a tester comes out clean when inserted into the cake layer that forms on top. Be sure to avoid the pudding layer on the bottom when testing.

Lemon Pudding Cups

SERVES 8

1 cup	granulated sugar	250 mL
¼ cup	sifted all-purpose flour	50 mL
2 tbsp	vegetable oil	25 mL
Pinch	salt	Pinch
2 tbsp	grated lemon zest	25 mL
⅓ cup	freshly squeezed lemon juice	75 mL
3	eggs, separated	3
1½ cups	milk, scalded (see tip, page 86)	375 mL
	Whipped topping	

- *Preheat oven to 325°F (160°C)*
- *Eight ¾-cup (175 mL) custard cups, ungreased*
- *13- by 9-inch (3 L) baking pan*

1. In a medium bowl, combine sugar, flour, oil and salt. Add lemon zest and juice and mix well until blended.
2. In a small bowl, whisk egg yolks and milk. Pour into lemon mixture.
3. In a small mixer bowl, on high speed, beat egg whites until firm peaks form. Fold into lemon mixture. Spoon into custard cups, dividing equally. Place cups in baking pan set on oven rack and pour in hot water to a depth of about 1 inch (2.5 cm).
4. Bake in preheated oven for 35 to 40 minutes, or until a tester comes out clean when inserted into the cake layer that forms on top. Be sure to avoid the pudding layer on the bottom when testing. Serve warm or chilled. Top with a dollop of whipped topping.

Oatmeal Raisin Pudding

SERVES 8

2¼ cups	quick-cooking rolled oats	550 mL
¾ cup	packed brown sugar	175 mL
⅔ cup	raisins	150 mL
1½ tsp	ground cinnamon	7 mL
½ tsp	salt	2 mL
2	eggs	2
3½ cups	milk	875 mL
1 tbsp	vegetable oil	15 mL
1 tsp	vanilla	5 mL

- *Preheat oven to 350°F (180°C)*
- *8-inch (2 L) square baking dish, greased*

1. In a large bowl, combine oats, brown sugar, raisins, cinnamon and salt. Make a well in the center.
2. In another large bowl, whisk eggs, milk, oil and vanilla until blended. Pour into the well in the oat mixture, stirring until well combined. Spoon into prepared baking dish.
3. Bake in preheated oven for 50 to 60 minutes, or until firmly set. Serve warm, cutting into squares or rectangles.

Upside-Down Mocha Pudding

SERVES 4 TO 6

1 cup	sifted all-purpose flour	250 mL
¾ cup	granulated sugar, divided	175 mL
3 tbsp	instant coffee granules	45 mL
1½ tsp	baking powder	7 mL
Pinch	salt	Pinch
1	egg, lightly beaten	1
½ cup	milk	125 mL
¼ cup	butter or margarine, melted and cooled	50 mL
½ cup	unsweetened cocoa powder	125 mL
1¼ cups	boiling water	300 mL

- *Preheat oven to 350°F (180°C)*
- *6-cup (1.5 L) casserole dish, buttered*

1. In a large bowl, combine flour, ½ cup (125 mL) of the sugar, coffee granules, baking powder and salt.
2. In a small bowl, whisk egg, milk and butter. Add to flour mixture, mixing until blended and smooth. Spoon into prepared casserole dish.
3. In another small bowl, mix together cocoa and the remaining ¼ cup (50 mL) of sugar. Sprinkle over batter and pour the boiling water slowly over top.
4. Bake in preheated oven for 30 to 35 minutes, or until center springs back when lightly touched. Set on wire rack to cool slightly. Spoon into individual dessert dishes, spooning some of the sauce over each. Serve warm.

Orange Surprise Pudding

SERVES 6

2	eggs, separated	2
½ cup	granulated sugar, divided	125 mL
¼ cup	butter or margarine, softened	50 mL
¼ cup	frozen orange juice concentrate, thawed, undiluted	50 mL
½ tsp	vanilla	2 mL
2 tbsp	all-purpose flour	25 mL
¼ tsp	salt	1 mL
1 cup	milk	250 mL

TIP: Eggs separate more easily when they are cold.

- *Preheat oven to 325°F (160°C)*
- *Six ¾-cup (175 mL) custard cups, buttered*
- *13- by 9-inch (3 L) baking pan*

1. In a small mixer bowl, on medium-high speed, beat egg whites until foamy. Add 2 tbsp (25 mL) of the sugar, one spoonful at a time, beating until firm peaks form.

2. In a medium bowl, cream remaining sugar and butter until light and fluffy. Add egg yolks, orange juice and vanilla, beating until well blended. Stir in flour and salt, then slowly stir in milk. Gently fold in beaten egg whites until fluffy and smooth. Spoon into prepared custard cups. Place cups in baking pan set on oven rack and pour in boiling water to a depth of about 1 inch (2.5 cm).

3. Bake in preheated oven for 25 to 30 minutes, or until top springs back when lightly touched with fingertip. Run a knife around the edges and invert onto serving dishes. Best served warm, but also delicious served cold.

Grandma's Pear Pudding

SERVES 6

½ cup	butter or margarine	125 mL
1 cup	all-purpose flour, divided	250 mL
1	can (28 oz/796 mL) pear halves, drained and sliced, juice reserved	1
1 cup	packed brown sugar, divided	250 mL
½ tsp	ground ginger	2 mL
¼ tsp	salt	1 mL
¼ tsp	almond extract	1 mL
½ cup	quick-cooking rolled oats	125 mL

- *Preheat oven to 350°F (180°C)*
- *6-cup (1.5 L) casserole dish, ungreased*

1. In a medium saucepan, over low heat, melt 2 tbsp (25 mL) of the butter and slowly stir in 2 tbsp (25 mL) of the flour. Cook for about 1 minute, stirring constantly. Gradually stir in the reserved pear juice. Remove from heat and cool, stirring constantly until mixture is thick and smooth. Stir in ¼ cup (50 mL) of the brown sugar, ginger, salt and the sliced pears. Spoon into casserole dish.

2. In a medium bowl, combine the remaining flour and remaining brown sugar. Cut in the remaining butter until crumbly. Add the oats and mix together well. Sprinkle over pears.

3 Bake in preheated oven for 35 to 40 minutes, or until bubbly and topping is golden brown. Set aside to cool slightly on wire rack and serve warm.

Passover Pineapple Pudding

SERVES 8 TO 10

⅔ cup	butter or margarine	150 mL
1¼ cups + 1 tbsp	granulated sugar	315 mL
8	eggs	8
2	cans (each 19 oz/540 mL) crushed pineapple, drained slightly	2
4 cups	matzo farfel (see tip, below), soaked in water	1 L
½ tsp	ground cinnamon	2 mL

TIP: Matzo farfel is available in Jewish delis.

- *Preheat oven to 350°F (180°C)*
- *8-cup (2 L) round soufflé dish, greased*

1. In a large saucepan, melt butter. Remove from heat and mix in sugar. Add eggs, one at a time, mixing well each time. Stir in pineapple, mixing well to blend. Fold in matzo farfel and cinnamon and spoon into prepared soufflé dish.
2. Bake in preheated oven for 1 hour, or until golden brown. Serve warm.

Pineapple Pudding with Butterscotch Sauce

SERVES 6 TO 8

2	eggs	2
1 cup	granulated sugar	250 mL
1 cup	chopped nuts	250 mL
1 cup	canned crushed pineapple, drained, juice reserved	250 mL
¾ cup	all-purpose flour	175 mL
1 tsp	baking powder	5 mL
¼ tsp	salt	1 mL
Butterscotch Sauce		
1	egg	1
1 cup	packed brown sugar	250 mL
¼ cup	reserved pineapple juice	50 mL
¼ cup	butter or margarine	50 mL
2 cups	whipped topping	500 mL

- *Preheat oven to 350°F (180°C)*
- *9-inch (2.5 L) square baking dish, lightly greased*

1. In a large bowl, whisk together eggs and sugar until light and frothy. Stir in nuts and pineapple, mixing until well blended.
2. In a small bowl, sift together flour, baking powder and salt. Add to the egg mixture and mix until well combined. Spoon into prepared baking dish and bake in preheated oven for 35 to 40 minutes, or until golden brown. Set on wire rack to cool. Cut into squares.
3. *Prepare butterscotch sauce:* In a medium saucepan, combine egg, brown sugar, ¼ cup (50 mL) water, pineapple juice and butter. Cook over low heat until dissolved and smooth. Set aside to cool, then add whipped topping. Spoon over pudding cake squares. Place a dollop of whipped topping on top, if desired.

Clafoutis

SERVES 6 TO 8

4	eggs	4
½ cup	milk	125 mL
¼ cup	whipped topping	50 mL
2 tsp	vanilla	10 mL
½ tsp	ground cinnamon	2 mL
¼ tsp	ground nutmeg	1 mL
⅔ cup	self-rising flour	150 mL
2 tbsp	granulated sugar	25 mL
4 cups	small apples, peeled, cored and thinly sliced	1 L
1 tbsp	freshly squeezed lemon juice	15 mL
2 tsp	brown sugar (optional)	10 mL
	Confectioner's (icing) sugar (optional)	

VARIATION: A clafoutis is a French fruit pudding. This recipe is great with any type of seasonal fruit you prefer: we used plums instead of apples for the photo opposite page 160.

- *Preheat oven to 375°F (190°C)*
- *10-inch (3 L) quiche dish, buttered*

1. In a large mixer bowl, combine eggs, milk, whipped topping, vanilla, cinnamon and nutmeg, beating on medium speed until well blended and smooth. Add flour, then sugar, and continue beating until the mixture is thick and smooth.

2. Arrange apple slices in prepared baking dish in a single layer; sprinkle with lemon juice. Pour batter mixture evenly over apples and sprinkle with brown sugar, if desired.

3. Bake in preheated oven for 35 to 40 minutes, or until golden brown. Serve warm or at room temperature and sprinkle with confectioner's sugar, if desired.

Self-Saucing Plum Pudding

SERVES 6 TO 8

1 cup	all-purpose flour	250 mL
⅓ cup	granulated sugar	75 mL
1 tsp	baking powder	5 mL
1 tsp	baking soda	5 mL
¼ tsp	salt	1 mL
1½ cups	coarsely chopped red or purple plums (about 3 medium)	375 mL
½ cup	milk	125 mL
2 tbsp	butter or margarine, melted	25 mL
1 cup	apple juice	250 mL
½ cup	packed brown sugar	125 mL
1 tsp	ground cinnamon	5 mL
¼ tsp	ground nutmeg	1 mL

Preheat oven to 350°F (180°C)
- *8-cup (2 L) casserole dish, greased*

1. In a large bowl, combine flour, sugar, baking powder, baking soda and salt. Add plums and mix together until well combined.

2. In a small bowl, mix together milk and butter. Add to flour mixture and stir just until blended. Spoon into prepared casserole dish and set aside.

3. In a medium saucepan, over medium heat, combine apple juice and ½ cup (125 mL) water and bring to a boil. Stir in brown sugar, cinnamon and nutmeg, stirring until sugar is dissolved. Remove from heat. Pour hot mixture over batter in casserole dish.

4. Bake in preheated oven for 30 to 35 minutes, or until topping is golden brown and firm to the touch. Serve hot or warm.

Perfect Baked Custard (page 86) ➤

Quick Pumpkin Patch Pudding

SERVES 8

1	package (5 oz/135 g) vanilla instant pudding and pie filling mix	1
1½ cups	evaporated milk	375 mL
1	can (14 oz/398 mL) pure pumpkin purée	1
1 tsp	pumpkin pie spice	5 mL
2 cups	whipping (35%) cream, whipped, or vanilla ice cream	500 mL

1. In a large mixer bowl, combine pudding mix and milk and beat according to package directions. Chill in refrigerator for 5 minutes.
2. Stir in pumpkin purée and pumpkin pie spice until well mixed. Spoon into 8 individual dessert dishes or glasses and chill in refrigerator for 15 minutes or until ready to serve. Top each with a dollop of whipped cream or ice cream.

Norwegian Prune Pudding

SERVES 8

⅓ cup	granulated sugar, divided	75 mL
2 cups	fresh bread crumbs (about 4 slices)	500 mL
¼ cup	butter or margarine	50 mL
1	jar (27 oz/767 g) stewed prunes	1
½ tsp	ground cinnamon	2 mL
Pinch	ground nutmeg	Pinch
2 cups	whipping (35%) cream	500 mL

- *Eight ¾-cup (175 mL) custard cups or ramekins*

1. In a small bowl, mix 2 tbsp (25 mL) of the sugar with the bread crumbs.
2. In a small skillet, melt the butter. Add the crumb mixture and sauté over low heat, stirring constantly, until mixture is browned and crispy. Set aside to cool on wire rack.
3. Drain the prunes, setting aside ¼ cup (50 mL) of the liquid, and remove the pits.
4. In a large bowl, combine the prunes, reserved prune liquid, 1 tbsp (15 mL) of the sugar, cinnamon and nutmeg. Mix together to blend well.
5. In a small mixer bowl, on high speed, beat whipping cream and remaining sugar until stiff peaks form.
6. Layer the crumb mixture, prune mixture and whipped cream in the custard cups, beginning and ending with cream. Chill in refrigerator for at least 3 hours or until ready to serve.

◄ Easy Mocha Mousse (page 102)

Danish Rhubarb Pudding

SERVES 6

2 lbs	rhubarb, cut into ½-inch (1 cm) pieces (about 7 cups/1.75 mL)	1 kg
¾ cup	granulated sugar, divided	175 mL
1½ tsp	vanilla, divided	7 mL
3 tbsp	cornstarch, mixed with 3 tbsp to ¼ cup (45 to 50 mL) cold water	45 mL
1 cup	whipping (35%) cream	250 mL

TIP: You could also spoon the pudding into 6 individual serving dishes and top each with whipped cream.

1. In a large saucepan, over medium heat, combine rhubarb, 1½ cups (375 mL) cold water and ½ cup (125 mL) of the sugar. Simmer until rhubarb is soft. Stir in ½ tsp (2 mL) of the vanilla and the cornstarch-water mixture and cook, stirring constantly, until sauce is transparent and thick. Spoon into a glass serving bowl, cover and chill in refrigerator for 3 to 4 hours or overnight.

2. In a small mixer bowl, on high speed, beat whipping cream until soft peaks form. Add the remaining ¼ cup (50 mL) sugar and the remaining 1 tsp (5 mL) vanilla and beat until stiff. Spoon over pudding.

Western Raisin Nut Pudding

SERVES 6 TO 8

2 tbsp	butter or margarine	25 mL
1¾ cups	firmly packed brown sugar, divided	425 mL
1¼ cups	biscuit mix	300 mL
1 tsp	vanilla	5 mL
1 cup	raisins	250 mL
½ cup	chopped nuts	125 mL

TIP: Serve with your favorite sauce (see Sauces, pages 176–79).

- *Preheat oven to 350°F (180°C)*
- *8-inch (2 L) square baking pan, ungreased*

1. In a medium saucepan, over medium heat, combine 2 cups (500 mL) water, butter and 1 cup (250 mL) of the brown sugar. Bring to a boil, stirring, and boil for 5 minutes. Pour into baking pan.

2. In a large bowl, mix together biscuit mix, the remaining ¾ cup (175 mL) brown sugar, ⅓ cup (75 mL) water and vanilla. Add raisins and chopped nuts and mix well until thoroughly combined. Spoon over brown sugar mixture in pan.

3. Bake in preheated oven for 40 to 45 minutes, or until set and golden brown. The batter will sink into the liquid and spread out as it bakes.

Raspberry Tapioca Pudding

SERVES 6

1	package (10 oz/300 g) frozen sweetened raspberries, thawed	1
1	lemon peel strip (1 inch/2.5 cm)	1
1 cup	red grape juice	250 mL
1/3 cup	granulated sugar	75 mL
1/4 cup	quick-cooking tapioca	50 mL
1/2 cup	whipping (35%) cream	125 mL
2 tbsp	confectioner's (icing) sugar, sifted	25 mL

1. Pour raspberries into a strainer and reserve the juice, but throw away the seeds. Add enough water to the juice to make it 2 cups (500 mL). Pour into a large saucepan. Add lemon peel, grape juice and sugar. Bring to a boil over medium heat, then reduce heat to low and simmer, uncovered, for 10 minutes.

2. Remove the lemon peel and add the tapioca. Cook, stirring constantly, for 10 minutes. Spoon into 6 individual serving dishes, cover each tightly with plastic wrap and chill in refrigerator for 4 to 5 hours, or until set.

3. In a small mixer bowl, on high speed, beat whipping cream and confectioner's sugar until soft peaks form. Spoon over puddings.

Old-Fashioned Vanilla Pudding

SERVES 6

3 cups	milk	750 mL
3/4 cup	granulated sugar	175 mL
3 tbsp	cornstarch	45 mL
2	eggs, well beaten	2
1 tbsp	butter or margarine	15 mL
1 1/2 tsp	vanilla	7 mL

1. In a large saucepan, over medium heat, combine milk with sugar and cornstarch. Stir and cook until bubbly, then stir and cook for 2 more minutes. Remove from heat.

2. Gradually stir 1 cup (250 mL) of the hot milk mixture into the beaten eggs, then pour into the saucepan. Cook over medium heat until nearly bubbly, but do not boil. Reduce heat to low and cook, stirring constantly, for another 3 minutes. Remove from heat.

3. Stir in the butter and vanilla and mix until well blended. Spoon into 6 individual dessert dishes, cover each tightly with plastic wrap and chill in refrigerator for 4 to 5 hours or overnight.

Traditional Baked Rice Pudding

SERVES 4 TO 6

2¼ cups	milk	550 mL
½ cup	long-grain rice	125 mL
⅓ cup	granulated sugar	75 mL
¼ tsp	salt	1 mL
Pinch	ground cinnamon or nutmeg	Pinch
2 tbsp	raisins (optional)	25 mL
1 tsp	vanilla	5 mL

TIP: Serve warm or cold, plain or with some cream.

- *Preheat oven to 250°F (120°C)*
- *6-cup (1.5 L) glass casserole dish, buttered*

1. In prepared baking dish, combine milk, rice, sugar and salt. Fold in cinnamon until just blended.

2. Bake, uncovered, in preheated oven for 30 minutes. Remove from oven and mix well, then bake for another 30 minutes. Stir in raisins and vanilla and bake for 1½ hours, or until rice is tender and most of the milk is absorbed.

Rice Pudding (Kugel)

SERVES 6 TO 8

1½ cups	long-grain rice	375 mL
1½ tsp	salt	7 mL
6	eggs	6
⅓ cup	granulated sugar	75 mL
½ cup	raisins	125 mL
⅓ cup	shortening or margarine, melted	75 mL

TIP: A great substitute for potatoes or plain cooked rice!

- *Preheat oven to 375°F (190°C)*
- *8-cup (2 L) casserole dish, well greased*

1. In a large saucepan, over medium-low heat, combine 4 cups (1 L) water, rice and salt. Cover and bring to a boil, then cook for 10 minutes. Drain any remaining liquid.

2. In a large mixer bowl, beat eggs and sugar until well blended. Stir in rice, raisins and shortening and mix together until thoroughly blended. Pour into prepared casserole dish.

3. Bake in preheated oven for 25 to 30 minutes, or until set and nicely browned. Serve hot or warm, cut into squares.

Hawaiian Rice Pudding with Pineapple Sauce

SERVES 6

4 cups	milk, divided	1 L
3 cups	cooked long-grain rice	750 mL
2/3 cup	granulated sugar	150 mL
1/2 tsp	salt	2 mL
1	package (4 oz/125 g) cream cheese, softened	1
2	eggs	2
1 tsp	vanilla	5 mL

Pineapple Sauce

1/4 cup	packed brown sugar	50 mL
1 tbsp	cornstarch	15 mL
1 tbsp	butter or margarine	15 mL
Pinch	salt	Pinch
1	can (19 oz/540 mL) pineapple chunks, drained, juice reserved	1
1/2 tsp	vanilla	2 mL

1. In a large saucepan, over medium heat, combine 3 1/2 cups (825 mL) of the milk, rice, sugar and salt. Bring to a boil and cook for 15 to 20 minutes, stirring often, until mixture is creamy and thick.

2. In a medium bowl, beat cream cheese until smooth. Whisk in eggs and the remaining 1/2 cup (125 mL) milk, beating until well blended. Stir into rice mixture and cook over medium heat for 3 minutes. Stir in vanilla and spoon into 6 individual dessert dishes, dividing equally.

3. *Prepare pineapple sauce:* In a medium saucepan, over medium heat, combine brown sugar, cornstarch, butter, salt and reserved pineapple juice. Bring to a boil and cook for 2 minutes, stirring constantly, until mixture is thickened. Remove from heat and stir in pineapple chunks and vanilla.

4. Spoon sauce over each pudding dish. Cool slightly on wire rack before serving.

Hint of Orange Creamy Rice Pudding

SERVES 4

1/2	orange	1/2
2 cups	milk, scalded (see tip, page 86)	500 mL
1/4 cup	long-grain rice	50 mL
1/4 cup	granulated sugar	50 mL
1/4 tsp	salt	1 mL
1	egg yolk, lightly beaten	1
1/2 cup	light (5%) cream	125 mL
1/4 tsp	vanilla	1 mL

TIP: Top each dish with a dollop of whipped cream or sprinkle some granulated sugar and cinnamon on top.

- *Double boiler*

1. Pare the orange half so that the peel is in one long continuous spiral.

2. In the top of a double boiler, over gently boiling water, combine orange peel, milk, rice, sugar and salt. Cook for about 15 minutes, stirring occasionally, until rice is tender. Remove the orange peel.

3. In a small bowl, whisk egg yolk and cream. Stir in a small amount of the hot mixture, then pour into hot mixture and blend thoroughly. Cover and continue cooking for 45 to 50 minutes, stirring several times, until mixture thickens. Remove from heat and stir in vanilla.

4. Spoon into 4 individual dessert dishes or glasses. Serve warm or chilled.

Country Corn Pudding

SERVES 6 TO 8

2 tbsp	butter or margarine	25 mL
1	onion, chopped	1
4 cups	corn niblets, well drained	1 L
2 tbsp	yellow cornmeal	25 mL
2 tbsp	all-purpose flour	25 mL
4	eggs	4
3 cups	milk or half-and-half (10%) cream	750 mL
2 tbsp	chopped fresh parsley	25 mL
1 tsp	Worcestershire sauce	5 mL
¾ tsp	mustard powder	4 mL
½ tsp	salt	2 mL

- *Preheat oven to 350°F (180°C)*
- *8-cup (2 L) casserole dish, buttered*
- *Roasting pan*

1. In a skillet, over medium heat, melt the butter. Stir in chopped onion and sauté until softened, about 5 minutes.

2. In prepared casserole dish, mix together corn, cornmeal and flour. Mix well to blend. Add the onion mixture and mix to blend.

3. In a large bowl, whisk eggs, milk, parsley, Worcestershire sauce, mustard and salt. Mix well and then add to corn mixture, stirring until well combined. Place casserole dish into roasting pan set on oven rack and pour in hot water until it reaches halfway up the sides of the baking dish.

4. Bake in preheated oven for 50 to 55 minutes, or until pudding is just set and the top is golden brown. Cool in the roasting pan for about 10 minutes, then remove casserole dish to wire rack. Serve hot or warm.

Matzo Meal Pudding

SERVES 4 TO 6

2	eggs	2
½ cup	granulated sugar	125 mL
2 cups	milk	500 mL
¼ cup	butter, melted	50 mL
1 cup	matzo meal (available at Jewish delis)	250 mL
2 tbsp	brandy	25 mL
½ tsp	salt	2 mL

TIP: Serve this pudding as a side dish in place of rice or potatoes.

- *Preheat oven to 350°F (180°C)*
- *8-cup (2 L) casserole dish, buttered*

1. In a large mixer bowl, on medium speed, beat eggs and sugar well until light and fluffy. Stir in milk and butter, mixing together to blend. Add matzo meal, brandy and salt, beating well to blend. Spoon into prepared casserole dish.

2. Bake in preheated oven for 1 hour, or until top is golden brown and pudding is set.

Cabbage Pudding (Kugel)

SERVES 6 TO 8

¼ cup	shortening or butter	50 mL
4 cups	finely shredded cabbage (about 6 oz/175 g)	1 L
1 cup	boiling water	250 mL
8	slices white bread, crusts removed	8
4	eggs, separated	4
½ cup	sifted all-purpose flour	125 mL
½ cup	blanched almonds, ground	125 mL
¼ cup	raisins	50 mL
2 tsp	freshly squeezed lemon juice	10 mL
1 tsp	salt	5 mL

- 8-cup (2 L) casserole dish, greased

1. In a skillet, over low heat, melt shortening. Add cabbage and cook for 45 to 50 minutes, stirring often. Chill for 3 to 4 hours or overnight. Meanwhile, preheat oven to 350°F (180°C).
2. Pour boiling water into a large bowl and add the bread slices. Soak bread for about 5 minutes, drain and mash.
3. In another large bowl, combine egg yolks, flour, almonds, raisins, lemon juice and salt. Add the bread and mix until well blended and very smooth. Add the cabbage and mix together lightly.
4. In a small mixer bowl, beat egg whites on high speed until stiff peaks form. Carefully fold egg whites into cabbage mixture until thoroughly blended. Pour into prepared casserole dish.
5. Bake in preheated oven for 30 to 35 minutes, or until set and golden brown. Cool on wire rack.

Potato Pudding (Kugel)

SERVES 6 TO 8

6	large potatoes, peeled	6
2	egg yolks, lightly beaten	2
1	onion, grated	1
¼ cup	matzo meal (available at Jewish delis)	50 mL
1½ tsp	salt	7 mL
1 tsp	baking powder	5 mL
¼ tsp	ground black pepper	1 mL
¼ cup	butter or shortening, melted, divided	50 mL
2	egg whites	2

TIP: Serve hot or warm alongside chicken or meat dishes.

- *Preheat oven to 375°F (190°C)*
- *6-cup (1.5 L) casserole dish, greased*

1. Grate the potatoes into a large bowl of salted water. Drain well.
2. In the same large bowl, combine potatoes, egg yolks, onion, matzo meal, salt, baking powder and pepper. Add 2 tbsp (25 mL) of the melted butter and mix together until well combined.
3. In a small mixer bowl, on high speed, beat egg whites until stiff peaks form. Carefully fold into potato mixture until well blended. Spoon into prepared casserole dish and spoon the remaining 2 tbsp (25 mL) melted butter over top.
4. Bake in preheated oven for 1 hour, or until set and golden brown on top.

Sour Cream Noodle Pudding

SERVES 10 TO 12

1	package (12 oz/375 g) medium noodles or broad egg noodles	1
3	eggs	3
½ cup	milk	125 mL
1 cup	sour cream	250 mL
1 cup	creamy cottage cheese (about 8 oz/250 g)	250 mL
4 oz	cream cheese, softened	125 g
¼ cup	unsalted butter, melted, divided	50 mL
1 cup	raisins (golden or dark)	250 mL
½ tsp	ground cinnamon	2 mL
	Salt, to taste	

TIP: If not serving immediately, cool pudding completely in baking dish, cover tightly with plastic wrap and refrigerate.

- *Preheat oven to 350°F (180°C)*
- *13- by 9-inch (3 L) baking dish, ungreased*

1. In a large saucepan, bring salted water to a boil. Add noodles and cook until just tender, about 10 minutes. Drain and set aside.

2. In a large bowl, whisk eggs and milk. Add the sour cream, cottage cheese, cream cheese and 2 tbsp (25 mL) of the butter. Add the noodles, raisins, cinnamon and salt. Mix together until well blended.

3. Grease baking dish with the remaining 2 tbsp (25 mL) butter. Pour in the noodle mixture, spreading evenly.

4. Bake in preheated oven for 45 to 50 minutes, or until top is lightly browned and pudding is set. Cool for 5 to 10 minutes on wire rack, then cut into squares for serving.

Sweet Potato Rum Pudding

SERVES 6 TO 8

2½ cups	milk	625 mL
3	medium sweet potatoes or yams, peeled	3
3	eggs	3
1 cup	granulated sugar	250 mL
½ cup	slivered blanched almonds	125 mL
2 tsp	ground cinnamon	10 mL
2 tbsp	butter or margarine	25 mL
½ cup	rum or bourbon	125 mL

TIP: Delicious served with turkey or ham!

- *Preheat oven to 300°F (150°C)*
- *8-cup (2 L) shallow casserole dish, buttered*

1. Pour milk into prepared casserole dish. Grate the sweet potatoes directly into the milk to prevent darkening.

2. In a medium bowl, whisk eggs; gradually add sugar, beating until blended. Stir in almonds and cinnamon and mix together well. Spoon into potato mixture and mix together until well blended. Dot with butter.

3. Bake in preheated oven for about 1½ hours, until golden brown and pudding is set. When ready to serve, spoon the rum over top.

Bread Puddings

continued on next page

B read puddings were originally made to use up stale bread, but it wasn't long before they became a favorite comfort food. In most recipes you have the option of using any kind of bread, including challah or raisin bread, cakes, bread rolls or even doughnuts, or a combination of these. They should be day-old and broken or cut into pieces or cubes.

Traditional Bread Pudding

SERVES 6

2	eggs, beaten	2
¼ cup	granulated sugar	50 mL
1 tsp	vanilla	5 mL
½ tsp	salt	2 mL
¼ tsp	ground nutmeg	1 mL
4 cups	milk, scalded (see tip, page 86)	1 L
3	slices day-old bread, cut into cubes (about 2 cups/500 mL)	3

TIP: Serve warm with whipped cream or your favorite sauce (see Sauces, pages 176–79).

- *Preheat oven to 350°F (180°C)*
- *8-cup (2 L) casserole dish, buttered*
- *13- by 9-inch (3 L) baking pan*

1. In a large bowl, combine eggs, sugar, vanilla, salt and nutmeg. Mix well to blend. Add scalded milk and mix until thoroughly blended.

2. Stir in bread cubes and mix until well combined. Pour into prepared casserole dish. Place casserole dish in baking pan set on oven rack and pour in hot water to a depth of about 1 inch (2.5 cm).

3. Bake in preheated oven for 45 to 50 minutes, or until a knife inserted in the center comes out clean and dry. Cool on a wire rack.

Mock Bread Pudding

SERVES 6

1	egg	1
1½ cups	milk	375 mL
½ cup	granulated sugar	125 mL
2 tbsp	butter or margarine, melted	25 mL
3 cups	granola cereal (with or without raisins)	750 mL

- *Preheat oven to 350°F (180°C)*
- *Six ¾-cup (175 mL) custard cups or ramekins*

1. In a large bowl, whisk together egg, milk, sugar and butter until thoroughly blended. Add cereal and mix well. Spoon into custard cups.

2. Bake in preheated oven for 20 to 25 minutes, or until pudding is not liquid in the center but is still a bit jiggly. Serve warm.

Special Bread Pudding Cake

SERVES 10 TO 12

6	eggs	6
4 cups	milk	1 L
1½ cups	granulated sugar	375 mL
3 tbsp	vanilla	45 mL
1 tbsp	ground cinnamon	15 mL
1 tbsp	ground nutmeg	15 mL
2 tsp	minced orange zest	10 mL
2	large loaves (each 1 lb/450 g) French bread, cut into ½-inch (1 cm) cubes	2
1 cup	raisins	250 mL
1 cup	chopped pecans	250 mL

TIP: Serve warm or cold, with ice cream or your favorite sauce (see Sauces, pages 176–79).

- *10-inch (25 cm) springform pan, oiled, with outside covered with foil to seal*
- *Roasting pan*

1. In a large bowl, whisk together eggs, milk and sugar to blend. Add vanilla, cinnamon, nutmeg and zest and whisk until thoroughly blended.

2. Press one layer of bread cubes into the bottom of prepared springform pan so that there are no empty spaces between. Sprinkle some of the raisins and pecans on top.

3. Spoon one-third of the egg mixture over raisins and pecans and carefully press down into the bread cubes with your fingertips. Repeat layers until all of the bread cubes and egg mixture are used up. (Some of the egg custard mixture may be left over once the pan is filled, but continue to add it, a little at a time, pressing firmly into the bread cubes until all of the mixture is used up.) For best results, chill in refrigerator overnight. Meanwhile, preheat oven to 375°F (190°C).

4. Place springform pan in roasting pan set on oven rack and pour in water to a depth of about 1 inch (2.5 cm). Bake in preheated oven for 1 to 1½ hours, or until a toothpick inserted in the center comes out clean and dry. Cool slightly on wire rack and cut into slices.

Bread Pudding with Lemon Sauce

SERVES 4 TO 6

3	slices day-old bread, crusts removed, cut into cubes (about 2 cups/500 mL)	3
2 cups	milk	500 mL
¼ cup	granulated sugar	50 mL
3 tbsp	butter	45 mL
Pinch	salt	Pinch
2	eggs	2
½ tsp	vanilla	2 mL

Lemon Sauce

½ cup	granulated sugar	125 mL
1 tbsp	cornstarch	15 mL
Pinch	salt	Pinch
1 to 2 tsp	grated lemon zest	5 to 10 mL
2 tbsp	butter	25 mL
1 tbsp	freshly squeezed lemon juice	15 mL
	1 to 2 drops of yellow food coloring (optional)	

- *Preheat oven to 350°F (180°C)*
- *6-cup (1.5 L) casserole dish, greased*
- *13- by 9-inch (3 L) baking pan*

1. Spoon the bread cubes into prepared casserole dish. Set aside.

2. In a medium saucepan, over low heat, combine milk, sugar, butter and salt, heating just until butter has melted.

3. In a medium bowl, whisk eggs and vanilla. Whisk in the heated milk mixture until well blended. Spoon over bread cubes. Place casserole dish in baking pan set on oven rack and pour in water to a depth of about 1 inch (2.5 cm).

4. Bake, uncovered, in preheated oven for 40 to 50 minutes, or until a knife inserted near the edge of the pan comes out clean and dry. Cool on a wire rack.

5. *Prepare lemon sauce:* In a medium saucepan, over medium heat, combine sugar, cornstarch and salt and mix to blend. Stir in 1 cup (250 mL) water and zest and bring to a boil, cooking and stirring for 2 minutes. Remove from heat and add butter, lemon juice and food coloring, if using. Stir until well blended. Serve warm or cold over pudding.

Bread Pudding with Rum Sauce

SERVES 6 TO 8

4	slices day-old bread, crusts removed	4
¼ cup	butter or margarine, softened	50 mL
2	eggs, lightly beaten	2
2½ cups	milk	625 mL
½ cup	packed brown sugar	125 mL
½ cup	raisins	125 mL
1 tsp	vanilla	5 mL
Pinch	salt	Pinch
½ tsp	granulated sugar	2 mL
½ tsp	ground cinnamon	2 mL

Rum Sauce

1½ cups	granulated sugar	375 mL
1½ cups	corn syrup	375 mL
2 cups	light (5%) cream, divided	500 mL
½ cup	butter or margarine	125 mL
3 tbsp	light rum	45 mL
½ tsp	vanilla	2 mL

- *Preheat oven to 350°F (180°C)*
- *8-cup (2 L) casserole dish, buttered*

1. Butter the bread slices and cut into cubes. Put cubes into prepared casserole dish.
2. In a large bowl, combine eggs, milk, brown sugar, raisins, vanilla and salt. Mix together to blend thoroughly. Spoon over bread cubes and sprinkle sugar and cinnamon on top.
3. Bake in preheated oven for 45 to 50 minutes, or until browned.
4. *Prepare rum sauce:* In a large saucepan, over medium heat, combine sugar, corn syrup, 1 cup (250 mL) of the cream and butter. Bring to a boil and cook without stirring to the firm-ball stage, 245°F (118°C) on a candy thermometer. Lower the heat and add the remaining 1 cup (250 mL) cream. Cook for another 15 to 20 minutes, or until golden brown. Remove from heat, add the rum and vanilla and mix well. Serve over warm or cold pudding.

Apple-Raisin Bread Pudding

SERVES 6 TO 8

7	slices raisin bread, toasted	7
1	can (19 oz/540 mL) apple pie filling	1

TIP: Serve with your favorite sauce (see Sauces, pages 176–79).

- *Preheat oven to 375°F (190°C)*
- *8- by 4-inch (1.5 L) glass loaf pan, ungreased*

1. Remove crusts from bread and cut 1 slice into 3 strips.
2. Line the bottom of the loaf pan with 2 slices of bread and 1 strip of bread. Spoon about ⅔ cup (150 mL) of the apple pie filling over top. Repeat with two more layers.
3. Bake in preheated oven for 40 to 45 minutes, or until browned. Serve warm.

Bread Pudding with Vanilla Sauce

SERVES 6

2 cups	milk	500 mL
1/4 cup	butter or margarine	50 mL
6	slices raisin bread, cut into cubes (about 4 cups/1 L)	6
2	eggs, lightly beaten	2
1/2 cup	granulated sugar	125 mL
1 tsp	vanilla	5 mL
1/2 tsp	ground nutmeg	2 mL

Vanilla Sauce

1/2 cup	firmly packed brown sugar	125 mL
1/2 cup	granulated sugar	125 mL
1/2 cup	butter or margarine	125 mL
1/2 cup	whipping (35%) cream	125 mL
1 tsp	vanilla	5 mL

- *Preheat oven to 350°F (180°C)*
- *6-cup (1.5 L) casserole dish, greased*

1. In a medium saucepan, over medium heat, cook milk and butter for about 5 minutes, or until butter is melted.
2. Put bread cubes in a large bowl. Pour milk mixture over bread and let stand for 10 minutes. Then add eggs, sugar, vanilla and nutmeg and mix to blend. Spoon into prepared casserole dish.
3. Bake in preheated oven for 45 to 50 minutes, or until center of pudding is set.
4. *Prepare vanilla sauce:* In a medium saucepan, over medium heat, combine brown sugar, granulated sugar, butter and whipping cream. Cook for 5 to 8 minutes, stirring often, until mixture comes to a boil and thickens. Stir in vanilla. Serve over warm pudding.

Egg Bread 'n' Butter Pudding

SERVES 6

3	eggs	3
2/3 cup	granulated sugar	150 mL
Pinch	salt	Pinch
2 cups	milk	500 mL
3 tbsp	butter or margarine, melted	45 mL
2 tsp	vanilla	10 mL
1 1/2 tsp	ground cinnamon	7 mL
Pinch	ground nutmeg	Pinch
	Finely grated zest of 1 lemon or orange	
6	slices stale egg bread (challah), cut into cubes (about 4 cups/1 L)	6
1/2 cup	raisins (optional)	125 mL

- *Preheat oven to 350°F (180°C)*
- *8-inch (2 L) square baking dish, buttered*
- *13- by 9-inch baking pan*

1. In a large bowl, whisk together eggs, sugar and salt until smooth. Add milk, butter, vanilla, cinnamon, nutmeg and zest. Mix thoroughly until well blended.
2. Place bread cubes in prepared baking dish. Pour egg mixture over top and mix well to coat all of the bread. Sprinkle with raisins, if using. Place baking dish in baking pan set on oven rack and pour in hot water until it reaches halfway up the sides of baking dish.
3. Bake in preheated oven for 55 to 60 minutes, or until golden brown and set in the center. Cool on wire rack.

Cinnamon-Raisin Bread Pudding

SERVES 12 TO 16

6	eggs	6
8 cups	milk	2 L
½ cup	granulated sugar	125 mL
2 tbsp	vanilla	25 mL
1½ tbsp	ground cinnamon	22 mL
½ tsp	ground nutmeg	2 mL
1½	loaves (each 1 lb/450 g) cinnamon-raisin bread	1½
2 tbsp	maple syrup	25 mL

- *Preheat oven to 350°F (180°C)*
- *13- by 9-inch (3 L) glass baking dish, greased*

1. In a large bowl, combine eggs, milk, sugar, vanilla, cinnamon and nutmeg, whisking until thoroughly blended.
2. Arrange 8 slices of bread in the bottom of prepared baking dish. Cut each remaining slice of bread diagonally in half and place in baking dish, overlapping slices.
3. Spoon egg mixture evenly over bread and press down with a spatula. Set aside for 15 to 20 minutes, or until bread slices have absorbed most of the egg mixture.
4. Bake in preheated oven for 50 to 60 minutes, or until golden brown, set and a knife inserted in the center comes out clean and dry. If topping begins to brown too quickly, cover loosely with a piece of foil for the last 15 minutes of baking.
5. Brush the top of the pudding with maple syrup and serve warm, or chill in refrigerator for 3 to 4 hours or overnight and serve cold.

Spicy Wheat Germ Pudding

SERVES 6

3 cups	fresh white bread crumbs (about 6 slices)	750 mL
3 cups	milk, scalded (see tip, page 86)	750 mL
3 tbsp	butter or margarine	45 mL
⅓ cup	wheat germ	75 mL
1 tsp	ground cinnamon	5 mL
¼ tsp	ground nutmeg	1 mL
Pinch	salt	Pinch
3	eggs	3
⅓ cup	firmly packed brown sugar	75 mL
1 tsp	vanilla	5 mL

- *Preheat oven to 350°F (180°C)*
- *Six ¾-cup (175 mL) custard cups, buttered*
- *13- by 9-inch (3 L) baking pan*

1. In a large bowl, combine crumbs, milk and butter and mix well. Stir in wheat germ, cinnamon, nutmeg and salt and mix together well. Let stand for 5 minutes, then beat until smooth.
2. In another large bowl, whisk eggs slightly. Add brown sugar, vanilla and bread mixture and mix thoroughly to blend. Set aside for 15 minutes, then spoon into prepared custard cups. Place cups in baking pan set on oven rack and pour in hot water to a depth of about 1 inch (2.5 cm).
3. Bake in preheated oven for 45 to 50 minutes, or until set and firm to the touch. Serve warm.

Whole Wheat–Yogurt Bread Pudding

SERVES 8

8	slices 100% whole wheat bread, toasted and cut in half diagonally	8
¼ cup	granulated sugar	50 mL
1½ tsp	ground cinnamon	7 mL
2	eggs	2
2 cups	skim or 1% milk	500 mL
1 tbsp	brown sugar	15 mL
1½ tsp	vanilla	7 mL
2	large apples, cored and diced	2
	Vanilla frozen yogurt	

- *Preheat oven to 375°F (190°C)*
- *9-inch (2.5 L) square baking dish, lightly greased*

1. Place half of the toasted bread slices in prepared baking dish.
2. In a small bowl, mix together sugar and cinnamon.
3. In a medium bowl, whisk eggs, milk, brown sugar and vanilla until well blended.
4. Sprinkle half of the cinnamon mixture and half of the apples over toasted bread in baking dish. Repeat the layers. Spoon egg mixture over top.
5. Bake, uncovered, in preheated oven for 45 to 55 minutes, or until set and a knife inserted in the center comes out clean and dry. Set aside to cool slightly on wire rack, then cut into squares. When ready to serve, top each square with a scoop of frozen yogurt.

Apple Pie Raisin Bread Pudding

SERVES 8 TO 12

3	eggs, well beaten	3
1	can (13.5 oz/385 mL) evaporated milk	1
1 cup	milk	250 mL
¾ cup	granulated sugar	175 mL
½ tsp	ground cinnamon	2 mL
¼ tsp	ground nutmeg	1 mL
1	can (19 oz/540 mL) apple pie filling	1
6 cups	fresh bread crumbs (about 12 slices)	1.5 L
1 cup	raisins	250 mL

- *Preheat oven to 350°F (180°C)*
- *12-cup (3 L) casserole dish, buttered*

1. In prepared casserole dish, combine eggs, evaporated milk, milk, sugar, cinnamon and nutmeg and stir until well blended. Add pie filling, bread crumbs and raisins and mix thoroughly. Set aside for about 10 minutes to allow bread crumbs to become saturated.
2. Bake in preheated oven for 40 to 45 minutes, or until golden brown and a knife inserted in the center comes out clean and dry. Cool on wire rack.

Applesauce Bread Pudding

SERVES 8

10	slices French bread (or other), cut into cubes, divided (about 6 cups/1.5 L)	10
1	jar (28 oz/796 mL) chunky sweetened applesauce	1
Pinch	ground nutmeg	Pinch
2	eggs	2
2 cups	milk	500 mL
½ cup	granulated sugar	125 mL
½ tsp	vanilla	2 mL
½ tsp	ground cinnamon	2 mL

- *Preheat oven to 325°F (160°C)*
- *11- by 7-inch (2 L) baking dish, greased*

1. Spoon half of the bread cubes into prepared baking dish. Spoon applesauce over top and sprinkle with nutmeg. Top with remaining bread cubes.

2. In a medium bowl, whisk eggs, milk, sugar and vanilla until well blended. Spoon over bread and sprinkle cinnamon over top.

3. Bake, uncovered, in preheated oven for 50 to 60 minutes, or until a knife inserted near the center comes out clean and dry. Cool on wire rack.

Apples 'n' Cheese Bread Pudding

SERVES 4 TO 6

2 tbsp	butter or margarine	25 mL
4	slices white bread, cut into cubes (about 3 cups/750 mL)	4
1	tart apple, peeled and thinly sliced	1
1 cup	shredded Monterey Jack cheese (about 4 oz/125 g)	250 mL
¼ cup	raisins (optional)	50 mL
1 cup	milk	250 mL
¼ cup	packed brown sugar	50 mL
½ tsp	ground cinnamon	2 mL
2	eggs, beaten	2

- *Preheat oven to 350°F (180°C)*
- *6-cup (1.5 L) casserole dish, greased*

1. In a skillet, on low heat, melt the butter. Add the bread cubes and mix together to coat cubes with butter. Cook, stirring, until cubes are toasted to a golden brown.

2. Spoon bread cubes into prepared casserole dish with the apple slices, cheese and raisins, if using, and mix together thoroughly.

3. In the same skillet, combine milk with brown sugar and cinnamon and scald (see tip, page 86). Remove from heat.

4. In a small bowl, whisk eggs. Pour the scalded milk mixture into the eggs, then spoon the egg mixture over the bread mixture.

5. Bake in preheated oven for 50 to 60 minutes, or until browned and firm to the touch. Cool on wire rack.

Slow Cooker Apple Bread Pudding

SERVES 8 TO 10

8	slices raisin bread, cut into cubes (about 5 cups/1.25 mL)	8
2	medium tart apples, peeled and sliced	2
1 cup	chopped pecans, toasted	250 mL
1 cup	granulated sugar	250 mL
1½ tsp	ground cinnamon	7 mL
½ tsp	ground nutmeg	2 mL
3	eggs, beaten	3
2 cups	half-and-half (10%) cream	500 mL
¼ cup	butter or margarine, melted	50 mL
¼ cup	apple juice	50 mL

- *Slow cooker, greased*

1. In a large bowl, combine bread cubes, apples and pecans. Mix well to blend. Spoon into prepared slow cooker.
2. In the same bowl, combine sugar, cinnamon and nutmeg, mixing to blend. Add eggs, cream, butter and apple juice, mixing until thoroughly blended. Spoon over bread mixture.
3. Cook, covered, on low setting for 3 to 4 hours, or until a knife inserted in the center comes out clean and dry. Serve warm or cold.

Chocolate Bread Pudding

SERVES 6 TO 8

4	squares (each 1 oz/30 g) semi-sweet chocolate, cut into pieces	4
3 cups	milk, divided	750 mL
½ cup	granulated sugar	125 mL
¼ cup	butter or margarine	50 mL
8	slices egg bread (challah) or white, cut into cubes (about 5 cups/1.25 L)	8
2 tsp	vanilla	10 mL
1 tsp	ground cinnamon	5 mL
3	eggs, lightly beaten	3
½ cup	ground nuts, toasted (optional)	125 mL
	Whipped cream	
	Shaved chocolate or chocolate curls	

- *Preheat oven to 350°F (180°C)*
- *8-cup (2 L) soufflé dish or casserole dish, buttered*

1. In a large saucepan, over low heat, combine chocolate, 2 cups (500 mL) of the milk, sugar and butter, stirring constantly until butter and chocolate are melted. (Or use a microwave-safe dish and microwave on High for 9 minutes.)
2. Remove from heat and stir in bread cubes, the remaining 1 cup (250 mL) milk, vanilla and cinnamon. Add the eggs and stir until thoroughly blended. Stir in nuts, if using. Let stand for 5 minutes, stir, then spoon into prepared soufflé dish.
3. Bake in preheated oven for 45 to 50 minutes, or until a knife inserted in the center comes out clean and dry. Serve warm topped with whipped cream and shaved chocolate.

Banana Bread Pudding

SERVES 6 TO 8

¼ cup	butter or margarine, melted	50 mL
6	slices day-old sourdough bread (or French or other), cut into cubes (about 4 cups/1 L)	6
3	eggs, lightly beaten	3
2 cups	milk	500 mL
½ cup	granulated sugar	125 mL
2 tsp	vanilla	10 mL
1 tsp	ground cinnamon	5 mL
¼ tsp	ground nutmeg	1 mL
¼ tsp	salt	1 mL
1	firm banana, sliced	1

TIP: Serve warm with whipped topping or your favorite sauce (see Sauces, pages 176–79).

VARIATION: Mash a ripe banana and mix it in with the milk mixture.

- *Preheat oven to 375°F (190°C)*
- *8-cup (2 L) casserole dish, greased*

1. In a medium bowl, toss together butter and bread cubes. Pour into prepared casserole dish.
2. In the same bowl, combine eggs, milk, sugar, vanilla, cinnamon, nutmeg and salt. Mix thoroughly to blend, then gently add the banana and fold to combine. Spoon mixture over bread cubes and stir gently, just enough to coat bread.
3. Bake, uncovered, in preheated oven for 40 to 45 minutes, or until firm and a knife inserted in the center comes out clean and dry. Cool slightly on wire rack.

Cornbread Cranberry Bread Pudding

SERVES 6 TO 8

8	slices cornbread (or other), cut into cubes (about 5 cups/1.25 L)	8
2	eggs	2
1 cup	whole cranberry sauce	250 mL
2 tsp	grated orange zest	10 mL
1 cup	freshly squeezed orange juice	250 mL
1 cup	milk	250 mL
½ cup	granulated sugar	125 mL
½ cup	chopped walnuts	125 mL
½ tsp	ground cardamom	2 mL
½ tsp	vanilla	2 mL
¼ tsp	ground ginger	1 mL

- *Preheat oven to 350°F (180°C)*
- *6-cup (1.5 L) casserole dish, greased*

1. Place cornbread cubes into prepared casserole dish.
2. In a large bowl, whisk eggs, then stir in cranberry sauce, orange zest, orange juice, milk, sugar, walnuts, cardamom, vanilla and ginger. Mix well until thoroughly combined. Pour over cornbread cubes and mix well, tossing to coat cubes. Let stand for 15 to 20 minutes, stirring occasionally, until liquid is absorbed.
3. Bake in preheated oven for 45 to 50 minutes, or until golden brown and a knife inserted in the center comes out clean and dry. Cool on wire rack.

Creamy Blueberry Bread Pudding

SERVES 6

4	slices day-old Italian bread (or French, brioche or other), cut into cubes (about 3 cups/750 mL)	4
2	egg yolks	2
½ cup	whipping (35%) cream	125 mL
⅓ cup + 1 tbsp	milk	90 mL
¼ cup	granulated sugar	50 mL
¼ cup	butter or margarine, melted	50 mL
½ tsp	ground cinnamon	2 mL
½ tsp	vanilla	2 mL
¼ tsp	ground nutmeg	1 mL
1 cup	fresh or frozen blueberries (about 6 oz/175 g)	250 mL
	Sifted confectioner's (icing) sugar	

- 8-cup (2 L) casserole dish, greased

1. Place bread cubes into prepared casserole dish.

2. In a large bowl, whisk egg yolks, whipping cream, milk, sugar, butter, cinnamon, vanilla and nutmeg until thoroughly blended. Add blueberries and stir until blended. Spoon over bread cubes, cover tightly with plastic wrap and chill in refrigerator for 30 minutes. Meanwhile, preheat oven to 350°F (180°C).

3. Bake, uncovered, in preheated oven for 25 to 30 minutes, or until golden brown and a knife inserted in the center comes out clean and dry. Sprinkle with confectioner's sugar.

Custard Bread Pudding

SERVES 6 TO 8

6	eggs	6
4 cups	warm milk	1 L
½ cup	granulated sugar	125 mL
½ tsp	ground nutmeg	2 mL
½ tsp	salt	2 mL
¼ tsp	vanilla	1 mL
2	day-old cinnamon buns, cut into cubes (about 3½ cups/875 mL)	2

- *Preheat oven to 350°F (180°C)*
- *8-cup (2 L) casserole dish, buttered*
- *13- by 9-inch baking pan*

1. In a large bowl, whisk eggs into milk, mixing well. Add sugar, nutmeg, salt and vanilla, whisking until well blended.

2. Place cubed buns into prepared casserole dish and pour in egg mixture, stirring until well combined. Place casserole dish in baking pan set on oven rack and pour in hot water until it reaches halfway up the sides of casserole dish.

3. Bake in preheated oven for 50 to 60 minutes, or until a knife inserted in the center comes out clean and dry and pudding is firm to the touch. Cool on wire rack.

Touch of Lemon Bread Pudding

SERVES 6

6	slices day-old bread, cut into cubes (about 4 cups/1 L)	6
3	eggs, lightly beaten	3
3 cups	milk	750 mL
½ cup	granulated sugar	125 mL
½ cup	raisins	125 mL
2 tbsp	butter or margarine, melted	25 mL
¼ tsp	salt	1 mL
	Grated zest of 1 lemon	
	Ground nutmeg	

- *Preheat oven to 350°F (180°C)*
- *Baking sheet*
- *6-cup (1.5 L) casserole dish, buttered*
- *13- by 9-inch (3 L) baking pan*

1. Arrange bread cubes on baking sheet in a single layer. Bake in preheated oven for 10 minutes to dry them.
2. In a large bowl, combine eggs, milk, sugar, raisins, butter, salt and zest. Mix well until sugar is dissolved.
3. Place bread cubes in a large bowl. Pour milk mixture over top and mix well. Let stand for 10 minutes to soak. Spoon into prepared casserole dish. Sprinkle nutmeg over top. Place casserole dish in baking pan set on oven rack and pour in hot water to a depth of about 1 inch (2.5 cm).
4. Bake, uncovered, at 350°F (180°C) for 55 to 60 minutes, or until set and a knife inserted in the center comes out clean and dry. Remove casserole dish from pan and set aside to cool slightly on wire rack. Serve warm.

Rhubarb Puff Pudding

SERVES 6 TO 8

8	slices day-old French bread, cut into cubes (about 5 cups/1.25 L)	8
3 cups	sliced fresh or frozen rhubarb (about 15 oz/450 g)	750 mL
3	eggs	3
1	can (13.5 oz/385 mL) evaporated milk	1
½ cup	granulated sugar	125 mL
1 tsp	grated orange zest	5 mL
1 tsp	ground cinnamon	5 mL
1 tsp	vanilla	5 mL
¼ cup	packed brown sugar	50 mL
	Whipped cream	

- *Preheat oven to 350°F (180°C)*
- *11- by 7-inch (2 L) baking dish, greased*

1. Place bread cubes and rhubarb in prepared baking dish and mix together to blend.
2. In a large bowl, whisk together eggs, evaporated milk, 1 cup (250 mL) water, sugar, zest, cinnamon and vanilla until thoroughly combined. Pour evenly over bread mixture and let stand for 10 to 15 minutes, or until bread has absorbed egg mixture.
3. Bake in preheated oven for 50 to 60 minutes, or until set and a knife inserted in center comes out clean and dry. Remove from oven and sprinkle brown sugar evenly over top. Put under broiler and broil for 1 to 2 minutes, or until brown sugar melts and the top is golden brown. Watch very closely. Serve warm with whipped cream.

Orange Marmalade Bread Pudding

SERVES 6

6	slices white bread (about 4 cups/1 L)	6
	Butter or margarine for spreading	
	Orange marmalade for spreading	
2	eggs	2
¼ cup	granulated sugar	50 mL
3 cups	milk, scalded (see tip, page 86)	750 mL
Pinch	salt	Pinch

VARIATION: Use any flavor of marmalade or jam you prefer.

- *Preheat oven to 300°F (150°C)*
- *6-cup (1.5 L) casserole dish, ungreased*
- *13- by 9-inch (3 L) baking pan*

1. Spread each bread slice with butter, then marmalade. Cut the slices into cubes or finger-length pieces and place them in casserole dish.

2. In a medium bowl, whisk eggs and sugar until sugar is blended and dissolved. Add scalded milk and salt and whisk to blend. Pour over the bread pieces, mixing thoroughly to coat bread. Place casserole dish in baking pan set on oven rack and pour in hot water until it reaches halfway up the sides of casserole dish.

3. Bake in preheated oven for 40 to 50 minutes, or until pudding is firm in the center and golden brown. Remove casserole dish from pan and set aside to cool slightly on wire rack. Serve warm or cold.

Raspberry Bread Pudding

SERVES 6

6	slices day-old French bread (or other), crusts removed and cut into cubes (about 4 cups/1 L)	6
3	eggs	3
½ cup	granulated sugar	125 mL
2 cups	milk	500 mL
1 cup	fresh or frozen, partially thawed raspberries (about 6 oz/175 g)	250 mL
1 tbsp	butter or margarine, cut into small chunks	15 mL
	Additional granulated sugar (1 to 2 tsp/5 to 10 mL)	

TIP: Serve with whipped topping or your favorite sauce (see Sauces, pages 176–79).

- *Preheat oven to 400°F (200°C)*
- *6-cup (1.5 L) casserole dish, buttered*

1. Arrange bread cubes in prepared casserole dish.

2. In a small mixer bowl, on medium speed, beat eggs until foamy. Beat in sugar and then add milk and beat until well blended. Pour over bread in casserole dish. Place spoonfuls of the raspberries in several places over egg mixture. Press down with a spatula until bread is well moistened. Dot with butter and sprinkle with granulated sugar.

3. Bake in preheated oven for 40 to 50 minutes, or until a knife inserted in the center comes out clean and dry. Serve warm or at room temperature.

Peaches 'n' Cream Bread Pudding

SERVES 6

2 tbsp + 1 cup	granulated sugar,	25 mL + 250 mL
2 tsp	ground cinnamon	10 mL
2 cups	canned peaches, drained and diced	500 mL
3½ cups	whipping (35%) cream	825 mL
½ cup	half-and-half (10%) cream	125 mL
6	eggs	6
1 tbsp	vanilla	15 mL
1 tsp	ground cinnamon	5 mL
Pinch	ground nutmeg	Pinch
4	slices egg bread (or sourdough, French or challah), cut into cubes (about 3 cups/750 mL)	4
½ cup	raisins (optional)	125 mL

- *Preheat oven to 350°F (180°C)*
- *6-cup (1.5 L) casserole dish, greased*
- *13- by 9-inch (3 L) baking pan*

1. In a medium bowl, mix together the 2 tbsp (25 mL) of sugar and cinnamon until blended. Add peaches and toss to coat.

2. In a large saucepan, over low heat, mix together whipping cream and half-and-half cream, stirring constantly, until simmering.

3. In a large bowl, whisk eggs. Spoon a little of the heated cream slowly into the eggs, whisking well so the mixture does not curdle, then stir in the remaining cream. Stir in the 1 cup (250 mL) sugar, vanilla, cinnamon and nutmeg. Mix well.

4. Put bread cubes, peach mixture and raisins, if using, into prepared casserole dish. Pour the cream mixture over top and let stand for 15 minutes, or until cream has completely soaked into the bread. Place casserole dish in baking pan set on oven rack and pour in hot water until it reaches halfway up the sides of casserole dish.

5. Bake in preheated oven for 45 to 50 minutes, or until browned and firm. Remove casserole dish from pan and set aside to cool on wire rack. Serve warm.

Fresh Fruit Bread Pudding

SERVES 4 TO 6

4	slices white bread (or other), cut into cubes (about 3 cups/750 mL)	4
1 cup	fresh raspberries (about 6 oz/175 g)	250 mL
1 cup	fresh blueberries (about 6 oz/175 g) or any other fruit	250 mL
2	eggs	2
1 cup	milk	250 mL
2 tbsp	brown sugar	25 mL
	Whipped topping or ice cream	

- *Preheat oven to 350°F (180°C)*
- *6-cup (1.5 L) soufflé dish or baking dish, greased*

1. In a large bowl, mix together bread cubes, raspberries and blueberries. Toss together well and pour into prepared soufflé dish.

2. In a small bowl, whisk together eggs, milk and brown sugar. Pour over bread and fruit mixture.

3. Bake in preheated oven for 20 to 30 minutes, or until a knife inserted in the center comes out clean. Cool on wire rack and serve with whipped topping or ice cream.

Baked Pear Bread Pudding

SERVES 6

6	slices day-old egg or French bread, cut into cubes (about 4 cups/1 L)	6
1 cup	peeled and chopped ripe pears (about 1 medium)	250 mL
¼ cup	raisins or dried cranberries (optional)	50 mL
2	eggs, beaten	2
2	cans (each 13.5 oz/385 mL) evaporated milk	2
⅔ cup	firmly packed brown sugar	150 mL
4 tsp	vanilla	20 mL
2 tsp	ground cinnamon	10 mL
½ tsp	ground nutmeg	2 mL
½ tsp	salt	2 mL

- *Preheat oven to 350°F (180°C)*
- *8-inch (2 L) square baking pan, greased*

1. Place bread cubes, pears and raisins, if using, into prepared baking pan.
2. In a medium bowl, whisk together eggs, milk, brown sugar, vanilla, cinnamon, nutmeg and salt, beating until well blended. Spoon over bread mixture and toss lightly to coat. Let stand for 5 to 8 minutes, or until liquid is absorbed. Press down on bread cubes with a spatula to make sure all of the liquid has been absorbed.
3. Bake in preheated oven for 45 to 55 minutes, or until firm and golden brown on top. Serve warm.

Pumpkin Bread Puddings

SERVES 4

1	egg	1
1 cup	table (18%) or half-and-half (10%) cream	250 mL
¾ cup	cooked pumpkin purée, cooled	175 mL
⅓ cup	packed brown sugar	75 mL
1 tsp	ground cinnamon	5 mL
½ tsp	vanilla	2 mL
¼ tsp	ground nutmeg	1 mL
5	slices raisin bread, cut into cubes (about 3½ cups/875 mL)	5

TIP: Serve with whipped topping, ice cream or your favorite sauce (see Sauces, pages 176–79).

- *Bake at 350°F (180°C)*
- *Four ¾-cup (175 mL) custard cups or ramekins, greased*
- *13- by 9-inch (3 L) baking pan*

1. In a large bowl, whisk together egg, cream, pumpkin, brown sugar, cinnamon, vanilla and nutmeg until thoroughly combined.
2. Stir in bread cubes and toss together with egg mixture to coat. Let stand for 5 to 10 minutes, or until bread softens slightly and has absorbed egg mixture. Spoon into prepared baking cups. Place cups in baking pan set on oven rack and pour in hot water until it reaches halfway up the sides of cups.
3. Bake in preheated oven for 20 to 25 minutes, or until a knife inserted into the center comes out clean and dry. Remove cups from pan and set aside to cool on wire rack. Serve warm or cold.

Strawberry-Apricot Bread Pudding

SERVES 6 TO 8

10	slices white bread (or other), cut into cubes (about 6 cups/1.5 L)	10
2	eggs	2
2	egg yolks	2
¾ cup	granulated sugar, divided	175 mL
1 tbsp	butter or margarine, melted	15 mL
2 tsp	vanilla	10 mL
½ tsp	ground cinnamon	2 mL
Pinch	salt	Pinch
4 cups	milk	1 L
2	egg whites	2
1 cup	apricot preserves, divided	250 mL
½ cup	strawberry preserves	125 mL

- *Preheat oven to 350°F (180°C)*
- *8-cup (2 L) casserole dish, buttered*
- *13- by 9-inch (3 L) baking pan*

1. Place bread cubes in prepared casserole dish.

2. In a large bowl, whisk eggs, egg yolks, ½ cup (125 mL) of the sugar, butter, vanilla, cinnamon and salt until blended. Stir in milk. Pour over bread cubes in casserole dish. Let stand for 15 to 20 minutes, or until bread has absorbed milk mixture. Place casserole dish in baking pan set on oven rack and pour in boiling water to a depth of about 1 inch (2.5 cm).

3. Bake in preheated oven for 45 to 50 minutes, or until center is almost set and a knife inserted near the edge comes out clean and dry.

4. Meanwhile, in a small mixer bowl, on high speed, beat the egg whites until foamy. Add the remaining ¼ cup (50 mL) of sugar, one tablespoonful (15 mL) at a time, beating until stiff peaks form.

5. Remove casserole dish from pan and spoon ½ cup (125 mL) of the apricot preserves over the hot pudding. With a pastry bag, press puffs of the beaten egg white mixture on top of pudding, close together so that no pudding is visible. Place back in baking pan and bake for another 10 minutes, or until the peaks of the egg whites are golden brown. Set aside to cool completely on wire rack.

6. In a small saucepan, over low heat, melt the remaining ½ cup (125 mL) apricot preserves. In another small saucepan, over low heat, melt the strawberry preserves. Strain each through a sieve and set aside to cool slightly. When ready to serve, drizzle some of each melted preserve over top of the pudding.

Old-Time Tomato Bread Pudding

SERVES 6

2 cups	canned diced tomatoes	500 mL
½ cup	firmly packed brown sugar	125 mL
1 tbsp	freshly squeezed lemon juice	15 mL
¼ tsp	salt	1 mL
Pinch	ground black pepper	Pinch
6	slices white bread (or French or sourdough), cut into cubes (about 4 cups/1 L)	6
⅔ cup	butter or margarine, melted	150 mL

TIP: If you prefer, you can purée the tomatoes before adding them to the saucepan.

- *Preheat oven to 375°F (190°C)*
- *8-cup (2 L) glass casserole dish, lightly greased*
- *13- by 9-inch (3 L) baking pan*

1. In a medium saucepan, over medium-low heat, combine tomatoes, brown sugar, ½ cup (125 mL) water, lemon juice, salt and pepper. Simmer, covered, for 5 to 6 minutes.

2. Spread bread cubes evenly in prepared casserole dish. Spoon melted butter over bread cubes and mix together until well combined. Pour tomato mixture over bread, but do not stir. Place casserole dish in baking pan set on oven rack and pour in hot water until it reaches halfway up the sides of casserole dish.

3. Bake in preheated oven for 55 to 60 minutes, or until top of pudding is browned. Remove casserole dish from pan and serve immediately.

Special Sage Bread Pudding

SERVES 6 TO 8

6	slices day-old bread, cut into cubes (about 4 cups/1 L)	6
1 to 2 tbsp	vegetable oil	15 to 25 mL
1	stalk celery, chopped	1
1	onion, peeled and chopped	1
1	clove garlic, minced	1
1 tbsp	chopped fresh sage (or 1½ tsp/7 mL dried)	15 mL
½ tsp	salt	2 mL
¼ tsp	freshly ground black pepper	1 mL
2 cups	sliced mushrooms (about 10) (optional)	500 mL
3	eggs, lightly beaten	3
1½ cups	vegetable or chicken broth	375 mL
2	green onions, thinly sliced	2

- *Preheat oven to 350°F (180°C)*
- *9- or 10-inch (23 or 25 cm) pie plate, lightly greased*

1. Spread bread cubes evenly in prepared pie plate. Set aside.

2. In a skillet, over low heat, heat 1 tbsp (15 mL) oil. Add celery, onion, garlic, sage, salt and pepper. Cook, stirring, for about 5 minutes. Increase heat to medium-high. If you are using mushrooms, add another 1 tbsp (15 mL) of oil, then mushrooms, and mix together well. Cook for about 5 minutes, until browned. Pour over bread cubes.

3. In a small bowl, whisk eggs and broth. Spoon over bread cubes. Spread green onions over top.

4. Bake in preheated oven for 40 to 50 minutes, or until golden brown and a knife inserted near the edge comes out clean and dry. Let stand for about 15 minutes before slicing and serving.

Bacon and Egg Bread Pudding

SERVES 8 TO 10

8	English muffins, split in half, toasted and buttered	8
5	thin slices Swiss cheese, cut in half crosswise	5
10	thin slices American cheese	10
10	slices Canadian-style bacon, uncooked	10
6	eggs	6
3 cups	milk	750 mL
¼ tsp	salt	1 mL
Pinch	ground black pepper	Pinch
	Chopped fresh parsley	

- *12-cup (3 L) casserole dish, buttered*

1. On a cutting board, place 5 muffin halves, split side up. Make sandwiches with 1 Swiss cheese slice, 1 American cheese slice and 1 slice of bacon and top with another half muffin, split side down. Cut each sandwich in half.

2. Place the remaining 6 muffin halves, split side up, on the bottom of prepared casserole dish, cutting to fit. Chop the remaining bacon and sprinkle over arranged muffin halves. Top with remaining cheese slices, alternating slices and overlapping.

3. Place sandwich halves over cheeses, overlapping slightly with the cut sides facing down. Be sure to keep the sandwiches intact.

4. In a large bowl, whisk eggs, milk, salt and pepper until well blended. Pour over sandwiches, spreading evenly and pressing sandwiches with a spatula or the back of a wooden spoon so that the egg and milk mixture is absorbed. Cover tightly with foil and chill in refrigerator for at least 3 hours or until ready to bake. Meanwhile, preheat oven to 350°F (180°C).

5. Bake, uncovered, in preheated oven for 50 to 60 minutes, or until nicely browned. Garnish with parsley and let stand for 10 to 15 minutes before serving.

Spinach and Cheese Bread Pudding

SERVES 8

6	eggs	6
2 cups	1% milk	500 mL
¼ tsp	dried thyme	1 mL
¼ tsp	salt	1 mL
¼ tsp	freshly ground black pepper	1 mL
Pinch	ground nutmeg	Pinch
8	slices firm white bread (or egg bread), cut into cubes (about 5 cups/1.25 L)	8
1	package (10 oz/300 g) frozen spinach, thawed, squeezed dry and chopped	1
1 cup	shredded Monterey Jack cheese (about 4 oz/125 g)	250 mL

TIP: This is one of my very favorites. It's delicious for breakfast or lunch.

- *Preheat oven to 375°F (190°C)*
- *13- by 9-inch (3 L) baking dish, lightly greased*

1. In a large bowl, whisk together eggs, milk, thyme, salt, pepper and nutmeg until thoroughly blended.
2. Carefully fold in bread cubes, spinach and cheese until well incorporated. Spoon into prepared baking dish.
3. Bake in preheated oven for 25 minutes, or until golden brown, puffed and a knife inserted in the center comes out clean and dry. Let stand for 5 to 10 minutes and serve warm.

Steamed Puddings

These puddings require a little more effort, but they are well worth it. People used to make steamed puddings mainly on holidays, but all of the many different kinds are delicious and can be enjoyed all year round.

Steamed pudding is made in a well-buttered or oiled pudding mold, or in a container of your choice, such as an ovenproof bowl. The mold should not be filled to the top, but about three-quarters full to allow room for expansion. The mold must be covered; if your mold does not have a cover, use a double thickness of foil and tie it down with a string.

In most recipes, the mold is set into a large pot, such as a Dutch oven, with a tightly fitting cover. Set the pot on a burner and place the covered mold in the pot, raised slightly with a rack, a canning jar ring or crumpled-up foil shaped like a small round plate placed beneath it. Pour boiling water into the pot until it reaches halfway up the sides of the mold. Let the water in the pot boil gently, over low heat, and follow the instructions in the recipe.

Steamed Bread Pudding

SERVES 8 TO 10

5	eggs, beaten	5
2 cups	milk, divided	500 mL
1/3 cup	maple syrup	75 mL
1/3 cup	apple juice	75 mL
1/4 tsp	ground nutmeg	1 mL
10	slices white bread (or other), cut into cubes (about 6 cups/1.5 L)	10
6	dates, pitted and chopped	6
1/2 cup	raisins	125 mL

- *Preheat oven to 350°F (180°C)*
- *8-cup (2 L) pudding mold, well buttered or oiled*
- *13- by 9-inch (3 L) baking pan*

1. In a medium bowl, combine eggs, 1 cup (250 mL) of the milk, syrup, apple juice and nutmeg, whisking until blended and smooth.

2. In a small saucepan, scald the remaining 1 cup (250 mL) of milk (see tip, page 86). Stir into the egg mixture.

3. Put bread cubes, dates and raisins into prepared mold, filling about three-quarters full, and toss well to coat. Spoon in the milk mixture and press down lightly with a spatula to make sure bread mixture is coated. Place mold in baking pan set on oven rack and pour in boiling water until it reaches halfway up the sides of mold. Cover pan loosely with foil.

4. Bake in preheated oven for 55 to 60 minutes, or until set. Remove mold from pan and set on wire rack to cool, then loosen sides of pudding with a knife and invert onto a serving plate. Cut into slices and serve warm.

Clafoutis (page 128) ➤

Buttermilk Crumb Pudding

SERVES 4 TO 6

1 cup	granulated sugar	250 mL
3 tbsp	butter or shortening	45 mL
2 cups	fresh bread crumbs, toasted	500 mL
1 cup	raisins	250 mL
1½ tsp	ground nutmeg	7 mL
1 cup	buttermilk or sour cream	250 mL
1 tsp	baking soda	5 mL

TIP: Serve with whipped cream or your favorite sauce (see Sauces, pages 176–79).

- *6-cup (1.5 L) pudding mold, well buttered or oiled*
- *Large pot*

1. In a large mixer bowl, cream sugar and butter until light and fluffy. Stir in bread crumbs, raisins and nutmeg, mixing until well blended.

2. In a small bowl, mix together buttermilk and baking soda until smooth. Pour into creamed mixture and mix thoroughly. Spoon into prepared mold, filling about three-quarters full, and cover.

3. Place mold onto a rack set in large pot and pour boiling water into pot until it reaches halfway up the sides of mold. Cover pot. Keep water boiling over low heat and steam pudding for 45 to 50 minutes, or until pudding is firm to the touch and a knife or wooden skewer inserted in the center comes out clean and dry. Be sure water is at a continuous low boil.

4. Remove mold from pot and set on wire rack to cool, then loosen sides of pudding with a knife and invert onto a serving plate. Cut into slices and serve warm.

Steamed Apple-Carrot Pudding

SERVES 8 TO 10

1	egg, lightly beaten	1
½ cup	granulated sugar or packed brown sugar	125 mL
½ cup	butter or shortening	125 mL
½ cup	grated carrot (about 1 medium)	125 mL
½ cup	grated potato (about 1 medium)	125 mL
½ cup	peeled, cored and grated apple (about ½ medium)	125 mL
	Grated lemon zest (optional)	
1½ tbsp	freshly squeezed lemon juice	22 mL
1⅔ cups	all-purpose flour, divided	400 mL
1 tsp	baking powder	5 mL
1 tsp	ground cinnamon	5 mL
½ tsp	baking soda	2 mL
¼ tsp	ground nutmeg	1 mL
Pinch	salt	Pinch
½ cup	raisins	125 mL
½ cup	dried fruit, chopped	125 mL
⅓ cup	chopped nuts (almonds or walnuts)	75 mL
1 tbsp	lemon zest (optional)	15 mL

- 8-cup (2 L) pudding mold, well buttered or oiled
- Large pot

1. In a large mixer bowl, on medium speed, cream egg, sugar and butter, beating until light and fluffy. Stir in carrot, potato, apple and lemon juice and mix well to blend.

2. In a small bowl, sift together 1½ cups (375 mL) flour, baking powder, cinnamon, baking soda, nutmeg and salt. Mix well. Add flour mixture to creamed mixture, mixing until thoroughly blended.

3. In the same small bowl, toss raisins and dried fruit with the remaining 2 tbsp (25 mL) flour. Shake off excess flour and add to mixture with nuts and lemon zest, if using. Spoon into prepared mold, filling three-quarters full, and cover.

4. Place mold onto a rack set in large pot and pour boiling water into pot until it reaches halfway up the sides of mold. Cover pot. Keep water boiling over low heat and steam pudding for about 3 hours, or until pudding is firm to the touch and a knife or wooden skewer inserted in the center comes out clean and dry. Be sure water is at a continuous low boil.

5. Remove mold from pot and set on wire rack to cool, then loosen sides of pudding with a knife and invert onto a serving plate. Cut into slices and serve warm.

Mom's Carrot Pudding

SERVES 6 TO 8

1 cup	packed brown sugar	250 mL
1/2 cup	butter or margarine, softened	125 mL
1 cup	grated carrot (1 to 2 medium)	250 mL
1 cup	grated potato (1 to 2 medium), divided	250 mL
2/3 cup	raisins	150 mL
1/2 cup	currants or other dried fruit	125 mL
2 tbsp + 1 cup	all-purpose flour,	25 mL + 250 mL
1 tsp	ground cinnamon	5 mL
1/2 tsp	ground nutmeg	2 mL
1/2 tsp	ground cloves	2 mL
1 tsp	baking soda	5 mL

TIP: Serve with your favorite sauce (see Sauces, pages 176–79).

- *6-cup (1.5 L) pudding mold, well buttered or oiled*
- *Large pot*

1. In a large bowl, cream together brown sugar and butter until light and fluffy. Add carrot and 1/2 cup (125 mL) of the potato and mix well. Sprinkle the raisins and currants with the 2 tbsp (25 mL) flour and stir until well blended.

2. In a small bowl, sift together the 1 cup (250 mL) flour, cinnamon, nutmeg and cloves and add to the carrot mixture.

3. In another small bowl, dissolve the baking soda in the remaining 1/2 cup (125 mL) of potato and add to mixture. Mix together just until blended. Pour into prepared pudding mold, filling three-quarters full, and cover.

4. Place mold onto a rack set in large pot and pour boiling water into pot until it reaches halfway up the sides of mold. Cover pot. Keep water boiling over low heat and steam pudding for 3 hours, or until pudding is firm to the touch and a knife or wooden skewer inserted in the center comes out clean and dry. Be sure water is at a continuous low boil.

5. Remove mold from pot and set on wire rack to cool slightly (about 10 minutes), then loosen sides of pudding with a knife and invert onto a serving plate. Cut into slices and serve warm.

Steamed Chocolate Pudding

SERVES 6 TO 8

1 cup	granulated sugar	250 mL
½ cup	butter or margarine, softened	125 mL
2	egg yolks	2
2 cups	all-purpose flour	500 mL
2 tsp	baking powder	10 mL
Pinch	salt	Pinch
½ cup	milk	125 mL
2	squares (each 1 oz/30 g) unsweetened baking chocolate	2
¼ cup	boiling water	50 mL
2	egg whites	2
1 tsp	vanilla	5 mL

- *6-cup (1.5 L) pudding mold, well buttered or oiled*
- *Large pot*

1. In a large mixer bowl, on medium speed, cream sugar and butter until fluffy. Beat in egg yolks until light and fluffy.

2. In a medium bowl, sift together flour, baking powder and salt. Add to creamed mixture alternately with the milk.

3. In a small bowl, melt chocolate in boiling water.

4. In a small mixer bowl, on high speed, beat egg whites until stiff peaks form. Fold melted chocolate, egg whites and vanilla into the creamed mixture until thoroughly blended. Spoon into prepared pudding mold.

5. Place mold onto a rack set in large pot and pour boiling water into pot until it reaches halfway up the sides of mold. Cover pot. Keep water boiling over low heat and steam pudding for 2 hours, or until pudding is firm to the touch and a knife or wooden skewer inserted in the center comes out clean and dry. Be sure water is at a continuous low boil.

6. Remove mold from pot and set on wire rack to cool, then loosen sides of pudding with a knife and invert onto a serving plate. Cut into slices and serve warm.

Christmas Pudding

SERVES 12 TO 16

3	eggs, well beaten	3
2 cups	ground suet	500 mL
1 cup	firmly packed brown sugar	250 mL
1/3 cup	currant jelly	75 mL
1/4 cup	fruit juice	50 mL
1 cup	all-purpose flour	250 mL
1 1/2 tsp	ground cinnamon	7 mL
1 tsp	salt	5 mL
1 tsp	baking soda	5 mL
3/4 tsp	ground mace	4 mL
1/4 tsp	ground nutmeg	1 mL
1 1/2 cups	fresh or dry bread crumbs	375 mL
1 1/2 cups	raisins, cut up	375 mL
1 1/2 cups	currants	375 mL
3/4 cup	finely chopped candied citron	175 mL
1/2 cup	finely chopped walnuts	125 mL
1/3 cup	candied orange peel	75 mL
1/3 cup	candied lemon peel	75 mL

TIP: Serve with your favorite sauce (see Sauces, pages 176–79).

- *10-cup (2.5 L) pudding mold, well buttered or oiled*
- *Large pot*

1. In a large bowl, combine eggs, suet, brown sugar, jelly and fruit juice. Set aside.

2. In another large bowl, combine flour, cinnamon, salt, baking soda, mace and nutmeg. Mix well to blend. Stir in bread crumbs, raisins, currants, citron, walnuts, orange peel and lemon peel. Add egg mixture and mix thoroughly until well blended. Spoon into prepared pudding mold, filling three-quarters full, and cover.

3. Place mold onto a rack set in large pot and pour boiling water into pot up to the level of the rack. Cover pot. Keep water boiling over low heat and steam pudding for 3 to 4 hours, or until pudding is firm to the touch and a knife or wooden skewer inserted in the center comes out clean and dry. Be sure water is at a continuous low boil.

4. Remove mold from pot and set on wire rack to cool slightly (about 10 minutes), then loosen sides of pudding with a knife and invert onto a serving plate. Cut into slices and serve warm.

Traditional Steamed Plum Pudding

SERVES 16 TO 20

⅔ cup	chopped candied citron	150 mL
2 cups	raisins	500 mL
1¾ cups	chopped walnuts	425 mL
1 cup	chopped dried figs (about 6 oz/175 g)	250 mL
1 cup	chopped dried apricots (about 6 oz/175 g)	250 mL
1 cup	chopped pitted dates (about 6 oz/175 g)	250 mL
4	eggs	4
1 cup	firmly packed light brown sugar	250 mL
2½ cups	fresh white bread crumbs (about 5 slices)	625 mL
½ cup	ground suet	250 mL
½ cup	corn syrup or light molasses	125 mL
½ cup	brandy	125 mL
1 cup	all-purpose flour	250 mL
1 tbsp	pumpkin pie spice	15 mL
1 tsp	salt	5 mL

TIP: Serve with your favorite sauce (see Sauces, pages 176–79).

- *10-cup (2.5 L) pudding mold, well buttered or oiled and sprinkled with granulated sugar*
- *Large pot*

1. In a large bowl, combine citron, raisins, walnuts, figs, apricots and dates.

2. In a large mixer bowl, on high speed, beat eggs and brown sugar until fluffy, about 2 to 3 minutes. Lower speed and mix in bread crumbs, suet, corn syrup and brandy until well blended.

3. In a small bowl, sift together flour, pumpkin pie spice and salt. Stir into egg mixture, mixing well, and pour over the fruits and nuts, mixing until combined and well blended. Tap any excess sugar out of prepared mold, spoon in pudding mixture, filling three-quarters full, and cover.

4. Place mold onto a rack set in large pot and pour boiling water into pot until it reaches halfway up the sides of mold. Cover pot. Keep water boiling gently over low heat and steam for 5 to 6 hours, or until pudding is firm to the touch and a knife or wooden skewer inserted into the center comes out clean and dry. Be sure water is at a continuous low boil.

5. Remove mold from pot and set aside to cool in mold for about 30 minutes, then loosen sides of pudding with a knife and invert onto a serving plate. Cut into slices and serve warm.

Old-Fashioned Steamed Cranberry Pudding

SERVES 8 TO 10

⅔ cup	granulated sugar	150 mL
2 tbsp	shortening or butter, softened	25 mL
1	egg	1
2 cups	all-purpose flour	500 mL
4 tsp	baking powder	20 mL
Pinch	salt	Pinch
1 cup	milk	250 mL
1 cup	chopped fresh cranberries (about 4 oz/125 g)	250 mL
1 tsp	finely grated orange zest	1 tsp
1	orange, peeled, sectioned and finely chopped	1

TIP: Serve with whipped cream or your favorite sauce (see Sauces, pages 176–79).

- *8-cup (2 L) pudding mold, well buttered or oiled*
- *Large pot*

1. In a large mixer bowl, on medium speed, cream sugar and shortening. Beat in egg until smooth and fluffy.

2. In a medium bowl, combine flour, baking powder and salt, mixing to blend. Add flour mixture to creamed mixture alternately with the milk, beating on low speed just until incorporated. Gently fold in cranberries, orange zest and orange, stirring until well blended. Pour into prepared pudding mold, filling three-quarters full, and cover.

3. Place mold onto a rack set in large pot and pour boiling water into pot to a depth of 1 inch (2.5 cm). Cover pot. Keep water boiling over low heat and steam for 1 to 1½ hours, or until pudding is firm to the touch and a knife or wooden skewer inserted in the center comes out clean and dry. Be sure water is at a continuous low boil.

4. Remove mold from pot and set on wire rack to cool slightly (about 10 minutes), then loosen sides of pudding with a knife and invert onto a serving plate. Cut into slices and serve warm.

Date Nut Steamed Pudding

SERVES 6 TO 8

½ cup	granulated sugar	125 mL
3 tbsp	butter or margarine, softened	45 mL
1	egg	1
1 cup	freshly squeezed orange juice	250 mL
¼ cup	orange marmalade	50 mL
1 tbsp	grated lemon zest	15 mL
1 tsp	vanilla	5 mL
1½ cups	sifted all-purpose flour	375 mL
1 tsp	baking powder	5 mL
¾ tsp	baking soda	4 mL
½ tsp	ground cinnamon	2 mL
½ tsp	salt	2 mL
Pinch	ground mace	Pinch
1 cup	chopped pitted dates (about 6 oz/175 g)	250 mL
1 cup	chopped walnuts	250 mL
½ cup	chopped candied cherries (optional)	125 mL

- *6-cup (1.5 L) pudding mold, well buttered or oiled*
- *Large pot*

1. In a large mixer bowl, on medium speed, cream together sugar and butter until smooth. Add egg, orange juice, marmalade, lemon zest and vanilla, beating until well combined.

2. In a large bowl, sift together flour, baking powder, baking soda, cinnamon, salt and mace. Mix to blend. Stir in dates, walnuts and cherries, if using. Spoon into egg mixture and mix together until combined. Pour into prepared mold, filling three-quarters full, and cover.

3. Place mold onto a rack set in large pot and pour boiling water into pot until it reaches halfway up the sides of mold. Cover pot. Keep water boiling gently over low heat and steam pudding for 2 to 2½ hours, or until pudding is firm to the touch and a knife or wooden skewer inserted in the center comes out clean and dry. Be sure water is at a continuous low boil.

4. Remove mold from pot and set on wire rack to cool slightly (about 10 minutes), then loosen sides of pudding with a knife and invert onto a serving plate. Cut into slices and serve warm.

Steamed Coffee Pudding

SERVES 6

½ cup	granulated sugar	125 mL
½ cup	butter or margarine, softened	125 mL
2	eggs, beaten	2
1½ cups	all-purpose flour	375 mL
½ cup	raisins	125 mL
¼ cup	strong black coffee	50 mL
1 tbsp	milk	15 mL
1½ tsp	baking powder	7 mL

- *6-cup (1.5 L) pudding mold, well buttered or oiled*
- *Large pot*

1. In a large mixer bowl, on medium speed, cream sugar and butter until light and smooth. Beat in the eggs until light and fluffy. Stir in flour, raisins, coffee, milk and baking powder until well blended. Pour into prepared mold, filling three-quarters full, and cover.

2. Place mold onto a rack set in large pot and pour boiling water into pot until it reaches halfway up the sides of mold. Cover pot. Keep water boiling over low heat and steam pudding for 1 to 1½ hours, or until pudding is firm to the touch and a knife or wooden skewer inserted in the center comes out clean and dry. Be sure water is at a continuous low boil.

3. Remove mold from pot and set on wire rack to cool slightly (about 10 minutes), then loosen sides of pudding with a knife and invert onto a serving plate. Cut into slices and serve warm.

Applesauce Gingerbread Steamed Pudding

SERVES 10

1	package (14.5 oz/400 g) gingerbread cake mix	1
1 cup	sweetened applesauce	250 mL
1 cup	raisins	250 mL
	Warmed applesauce or whipped topping	

TIP: If gingerbread cake mix is not available, substitute 1 package (18 oz/510 g) spice cake mix. The flavor will be a little more mild.

- *Ten ¾-cup (175 mL) custard cups, well buttered or oiled*
- *Large pot*

1. In a large mixer bowl, on medium speed, combine gingerbread mix, applesauce and ¼ cup (50 mL) water, beating for about 2 to 3 minutes, or until well blended, scraping sides of bowl often. Stir in raisins. Spoon mixture evenly into prepared custard cups and cover tightly with aluminum foil.

2. Place cups onto a rack set in large pot and pour boiling water into pot up to the level of the rack. Make sure water is not touching cups. Cover pot. Keep water boiling gently over low heat and steam puddings for 30 minutes, or until puddings are firm to the touch and a knife or wooden skewer inserted in the center comes out clean and dry. Be sure water is at a continuous low boil.

3. Remove cups from pot and set on wire rack to cool slightly (about 10 minutes), then loosen sides of puddings with a knife and invert cups into glass serving dishes. Serve warm with some warmed applesauce or whipped topping.

Special Sliced Jelly-Roll Pudding

SERVES 10 TO 12

1	jelly roll, cut into 7 slices, each ½ inch (1 cm) thick	1
⅓ cup	butter or margarine	75 mL
⅔ cup	sifted all-purpose flour	150 mL
1 cup	milk	250 mL
4	eggs, separated	4
¼ cup	granulated sugar	50 mL
1 tsp	vanilla	5 mL
Pinch	salt	Pinch

TIP: Serve with a favorite sauce, such as lemon sauce (see recipe, page 141).

- *10-cup (2.5 L) heatproof mixing bowl, well buttered or oiled and sprinkled with granulated sugar*
- *Large pot*

1. Tap out any excess sugar from the prepared bowl and line the bottom and sides with jelly-roll slices.

2. In a medium saucepan, over low heat, melt butter. Remove from heat and add flour, then stir in milk slowly. Return to heat and cook for 2 to 3 minutes, stirring constantly, until the batter forms a thick, smooth ball that follows the spoon around the pan. Remove from heat. Add egg yolks, one at a time, beating with each addition. Add sugar, vanilla and salt and beat until well blended.

3. In a small mixer bowl, on high speed, beat egg whites until soft peaks form. Fold into the batter until well incorporated. Spoon over top of jelly-roll slices and cover.

4. Place bowl onto a rack set in large pot and pour boiling water into pot to about one-third the depth of the bowl. Cover pot. Keep water boiling gently over low heat and steam pudding for 2 hours, or until pudding is firm to the touch and a knife or wooden skewer inserted in the center comes out clean and dry. Be sure water is at a continuous low boil.

5. Remove bowl from pot and cool in bowl for 5 to 10 minutes, then loosen sides of pudding with a knife and invert onto a serving plate. Cut into slices and serve warm.

Graham Wafer Steamed Pudding

SERVES 6

2 cups	graham wafer crumbs (about 24 wafers)	500 mL
1 tsp	baking powder	5 mL
Pinch	salt	Pinch
1/3 cup	granulated sugar	75 mL
1/4 cup	shortening or butter, softened	50 mL
1	egg, separated	1
1 tsp	vanilla	5 mL
2/3 cup	milk	150 mL

TIP: Serve with whipped topping, ice cream or your favorite sauce (see Sauces, pages 176–79).

- *Six 3/4-cup (175 mL) custard cups, well buttered or oiled*
- *Large pot*

1. In a medium bowl, mix together wafer crumbs, baking powder and salt until well blended.

2. In a large mixer bowl, on medium speed, cream sugar and shortening. Add egg yolk and vanilla, beating until well blended. Stir in crumb mixture alternately with the milk, mixing thoroughly to combine.

3. In a small mixer bowl, on high speed, beat the egg white until stiff peaks form. Fold into mixture. Spoon mixture evenly into prepared custard cups and cover tightly with aluminum foil.

4. Place cups onto a rack set in large pot and pour boiling water into pot up to the level of the rack. Make sure water is not touching cups. Cover pot. Keep water boiling gently over low heat and steam puddings for 30 minutes, or until puddings are firm to the touch and a knife or wooden skewer inserted in the center comes out clean and dry. Be sure water is at a continuous low boil.

5. Remove cups from pot and set on wire rack to cool slightly (about 10 minutes), then loosen sides of puddings with a knife and invert cups into glass serving dishes. Serve warm.

Steamed Spicy Mincemeat Pudding

SERVES 6 TO 8

1	egg	1
1 cup	firmly packed brown sugar	250 mL
⅓ cup	butter or margarine	75 mL
1 cup	sifted all-purpose flour	250 mL
1 tsp	baking powder	5 mL
½ tsp	salt	2 mL
½ cup	milk	125 mL
1 cup	prepared mincemeat (from a jar)	250 mL
½ cup	dry bread crumbs	125 mL
½ cup	chopped walnuts	125 mL

- *4-cup (1 L) pudding mold, well buttered or oiled*
- *Large pot*

1. In a large mixer bowl, on medium speed, combine egg, brown sugar and butter, beating until smooth and fluffy.

2. In a small bowl, sift flour, baking powder and salt. Add flour mixture to egg mixture alternately with the milk, beating well after each addition. Gently stir in mincemeat, bread crumbs and walnuts, just until well blended. Spoon into prepared pudding mold, filling three-quarters full, and cover.

3. Place mold onto a rack set in large pot and pour boiling water into pot until it reaches halfway up the sides of mold. Cover pot. Keep water boiling gently over low heat and steam pudding for 1 hour, or until pudding is firm to the touch and a knife or wooden skewer inserted into the center comes out clean and dry. Be sure water is at a continuous low boil.

4. Remove mold from pot and set on wire rack to cool slightly (about 10 minutes), then loosen sides of pudding with a knife and invert onto a serving plate. Cut into slices and serve warm.

Steamed Pumpkin Pie Pudding

SERVES 6 TO 8

1½ cups	all-purpose flour	375 mL
½ cup	instant mashed potato powder	125 mL
2 tsp	pumpkin pie spice	10 mL
1 tsp	salt	5 mL
1 tsp	baking soda	5 mL
¾ cup	firmly packed brown sugar	175 mL
¼ cup	butter or margarine, softened	50 mL
3	eggs, separated	3
1 tsp	grated orange zest	5 mL
1 tsp	vanilla	5 mL
¾ cup	freshly squeezed orange juice	175 mL
1 cup	canned pumpkin purée	250 mL
½ cup	chopped walnuts	125 mL

TIP: Serve with whipped topping, a scoop of vanilla ice cream or your favorite sauce (see Sauces, pages 176–79).

- *8-cup (2 L) pudding mold, well buttered or oiled*
- *Large pot*

1. In a medium bowl, sift together flour, potato powder, pumpkin spice, salt and baking soda.

2. In a large mixer bowl, on medium speed, cream brown sugar and butter until fluffy. Beat in eggs, zest and vanilla until well blended. Add flour mixture alternately with the orange juice, beating well after each addition. Gently fold in pumpkin and walnuts. Spoon into prepared pudding mold, filling three-quarters full, and cover.

3. Place mold onto a rack set in large pot and pour boiling water into pot until it reaches halfway up the sides of mold. Cover pot. Keep water boiling gently over low heat and steam pudding for 2 hours, or until pudding is firm to the touch and a knife or wooden skewer inserted into the center comes out clean and dry. Be sure water is at a continuous low boil.

4. Remove mold from pot and set on a wire rack to cool slightly (about 10 minutes), then loosen sides of pudding with a knife and invert onto a serving plate. Cut into wedges and serve warm.

Sauces

Burnt Sugar Sauce

MAKES ABOUT 2 CUPS (500 ML)

1½ cups	granulated sugar	375 mL
1 cup	boiling water	250 mL

TIP: This is a great sauce for custards.

1. In a medium saucepan, over low heat, cook the sugar, stirring constantly with a wooden spoon, until the sugar is melted and becomes a golden syrup. Remove from heat.

2. Gradually, very slowly, add the water and stir until blended. Return saucepan to heat and continue cooking, over low heat, stirring constantly, until sauce is syrupy and smooth. The sauce will be thin but will get thicker as it cools.

Christmas Pudding Sauce

MAKES ABOUT 3 CUPS (750 ML)

¾ cup	butter or margarine	175 mL
1 cup	granulated sugar	250 mL
¼ cup	all-purpose flour	50 mL
2	eggs, separated (see tip, below)	2
1 cup	hot milk	250 mL

TIP: This recipe contains raw egg whites. If the food safety of raw egg whites is a concern for you, substitute 6 tbsp (90 mL) pasteurized egg whites, found in the refrigerated egg section of most supermarkets. Alternatively, omit egg whites and add ⅔ cup (150 mL) frozen whipped topping, thawed.

- *Double boiler*

1. In a large mixer bowl, cream butter until smooth. Add sugar and flour and beat until well blended.

2. In a small bowl, whisk the egg yolks until well beaten. Add to creamed mixture with the hot milk. Pour mixture into top of double boiler and cook over simmering water until mixture thickens. Set aside to cool.

3. In a small mixer bowl, on high speed, beat the egg whites until stiff peaks form. When ready to serve pudding, fold in the beaten egg whites.

Quick Custard Sauce

MAKES ABOUT 4 CUPS (1 L)

1	package (4 oz/113 g) instant vanilla pudding mix	1
4 cups	milk	1 L
2 tbsp	granulated sugar	25 mL
1 tbsp	butter or margarine	15 mL
½ tsp	vanilla	2 mL

1. In a medium saucepan, over medium heat, combine pudding mix, milk, sugar, butter and vanilla. Cook according to the directions on the pudding package. Remove from heat.

2. Spoon into a bowl, cover tightly with plastic wrap and set aside to cool. Can be served warm or cold.

Sour Cream Custard Sauce

MAKES ABOUT 2 CUPS (500 ML)

½ cup	granulated sugar	125 mL
2 tbsp	cornstarch	25 mL
¼ tsp	salt	1 mL
1½ cups	milk	375 mL
4	eggs, well beaten	4
½ cup	sour cream	125 mL
1½ tsp	vanilla	7 mL

1. In a medium saucepan, over medium heat, combine sugar, cornstarch and salt. Slowly stir in milk, mixing until smooth. Bring to a boil, stirring constantly. Stir a small amount of this hot mixture into the beaten eggs and return all to the saucepan, stirring constantly. Cook for 2 to 3 minutes. Remove from heat. Mix in sour cream and vanilla and mix well to blend.

2. Place saucepan in ice water and stir for 5 minutes. Transfer to a medium bowl, cover tightly with plastic wrap and chill in refrigerator for 3 to 4 hours or overnight.

Eggnog Sauce

**MAKES ABOUT
2¾ CUPS (675 ML)**

5	egg yolks	5
⅔ cup	granulated sugar	150 mL
½ tsp	grated fresh nutmeg	2 mL
2 cups	light (5%) cream	500 mL
1 tbsp	rum or brandy	15 mL
2 tsp	vanilla	10 mL

TIP: Great with custards and puddings.

1. In a medium bowl, whisk egg yolks, sugar and nutmeg.

2. In a medium saucepan, over medium heat, scald cream, heating until small bubbles form around the edges. Pour into egg mixture, whisking until blended, and return to saucepan. Continue cooking over medium heat, stirring constantly, until mixture is thickened.

3. Pour into a strainer set over a medium bowl and stir in the rum and vanilla. Cover tightly with plastic wrap and chill in refrigerator for 3 to 4 hours or overnight. Serve cold, or warm by microwaving on Medium for 3 minutes.

Fruit Cocktail Sauce

MAKES ABOUT 2 CUPS (500 ML)

1	can (14 oz/398 mL) fruit cocktail, drained, liquid reserved	1
1 tbsp	cornstarch	15 mL
1½ tsp	grated lemon zest	7 mL
2 tbsp	freshly squeezed lemon juice	25 mL

TIP: Wonderful served with all types of desserts, especially custards and puddings.

1. In a small saucepan, mix together 3 tbsp to ¼ cup (45 to 50 mL) of the reserved fruit liquid and cornstarch. Whisk until smooth and blended. Stir in the remaining fruit liquid and the lemon juice.

2. Bring to a boil over medium heat, stirring constantly, and boil for 3 minutes, or until sauce thickens. Remove from heat. Stir in lemon zest and fruit cocktail. Best when served warm.

Foamy Pudding Sauce

MAKES ABOUT 3 CUPS (750 ML)

1	egg (see tip, below)	1
⅓ cup	butter or margarine, melted	75 mL
1½ cups	confectioner's (icing) sugar, sifted	375 mL
1 tsp	vanilla	5 mL
1 tsp	rum extract	5 mL
1 cup	whipping (35%) cream	250 mL

1. In a medium mixer bowl, on medium speed, beat egg until thick. Add butter, beating until well blended. Mix in confectioner's sugar, vanilla and rum extract , stirring until well combined and smooth.

2. In a small mixer bowl, on high speed, beat whipping cream until stiff peaks form. Fold into egg mixture. Cover tightly with plastic wrap and chill in refrigerator for 3 to 4 hours or overnight.

Melba Sauce

MAKES ABOUT 1 CUP (250 ML)

1	package (10 oz/300 g) frozen red raspberries, thawed	1
⅔ cup	granulated sugar	150 mL
Pinch	cream of tartar	Pinch

TIP: Usually served on peaches and ice cream, but also delicious on puddings.

1. Place raspberries into a sieve set over a medium saucepan and press through, throwing away the seeds.

2. Add sugar and cream of tartar to raspberries and cook over medium-high heat to boiling, stirring constantly. Cook for about 3 minutes, or until the mixture is slightly thickened. Remove from heat and spoon into a bowl. Cover tightly with plastic wrap and chill in refrigerator for 3 to 4 hours or overnight.

Choice Pudding Sauce

MAKES ABOUT 3 CUPS (750 ML)

1 cup	packed brown sugar	250 mL
½ cup	butter or margarine	125 mL
2	egg whites, lightly beaten (see tip, below)	2
1 cup	whipping (35%) cream	250 mL

TIPS: A perfect sauce for any pudding or custard.

This recipe contains raw eggs. If the food safety of raw eggs is a concern for you, substitute 4 tbsp (90 mL) pasteurized eggs, found in the refrigerated egg section of most supermarkets. Alternatively, omit egg whites and use ⅔ cups frozen whipped topping, thawed.

- *Double boiler*

1. In the top of a double boiler, combine brown sugar and butter and cook over simmering water until the sugar is dissolved. Remove top of double boiler and add the beaten egg whites. Set aside to cool.

2. In a small mixer bowl, on high speed, beat whipping cream until stiff peaks form. Fold into the cooled mixture.

Mock Vanilla Ice Cream Sauce

MAKES ABOUT 2 CUPS (500 ML)

1	egg (see tip, at left)	1
3 tbsp	granulated sugar	45 mL
Pinch	salt	Pinch
1/4 cup	butter or margarine, melted	50 mL
1/2 tsp	vanilla	2 mL
3/4 cup	whipping (35%) cream	175 mL

TIP: Delicious on puddings and any other dessert that's great with real vanilla ice cream.

1. In a medium mixer bowl, on medium speed, beat egg, sugar and salt until fluffy but thickened. Beat in butter, a little bit at a time, until blended. Stir in vanilla.
2. In a small mixer bowl, on high speed, beat whipping cream until stiff peaks form. Fold into the egg mixture thoroughly until well combined. Chill in refrigerator until ready to serve.

Instant Pudding Sauce

MAKES ABOUT 4 CUPS (1 L)

1	package (4 oz/113 g) instant pudding mix (chocolate, vanilla or any other)	1
3 cups	milk	750 mL
1/4 cup	confectioner's (icing) sugar, sifted	50 mL
1 tsp	vanilla	5 mL
1/2 cup	whipping (35%) cream, whipped	125 mL

TIP: Especially good served on baked or steamed puddings.

1. In a large mixer bowl, combine pudding mix, milk, confectioner's sugar and vanilla. Beat on medium speed for 1 to 2 minutes, or until well blended and smooth. Fold in the whipped cream until well combined.
2. Cover tightly with plastic wrap and chill in refrigerator for at least 1 hour or until ready to serve.

Fresh Strawberry Sauce

MAKES ABOUT 2 CUPS (500 ML)

1/4 cup	margarine (no substitute)	50 mL
1 1/2 cups	confectioner's (icing) sugar, sifted	375 mL
1/4 cup	crushed fresh strawberries (about 3 berries)	50 mL

TIP: This is a great, classic sauce for steamed puddings.

1. In a medium mixer bowl, on medium speed, cream margarine until fluffy. Beat in confectioner's sugar, a little bit at a time, until blended and smooth. Add strawberries and continue beating until mixture is blended and smooth.
2. Cover tightly with plastic wrap and chill in refrigerator for 3 to 4 hours or overnight.

Index

National Library of Canada Cataloguing in Publication

Brody, Esther
    250 best cobblers, custards, cupcakes, bread puddings & more/Esther Brody.

Includes index.
ISBN 0-7788-0105-5

1. Desserts.
I. Title. II. Title: Two hundred fifty best cobblers, custards, cupcakes, bread puddings & more.

TX773.B76 2004   641.8'6   C2004-902922-3

More Great Books
from Robert Rose

Appliance Cooking

- 125 Best Microwave Oven Recipes
  by Johanna Burkhard
- 125 Best Pressure Cooker Recipes
  by Cinda Chavich
- The 150 Best Slow Cooker Recipes
  by Judith Finlayson
- Delicious & Dependable Slow Cooker Recipes
  by Judith Finlayson
- 125 Best Vegetarian Slow Cooker Recipes
  by Judith Finlayson
- America's Best Slow Cooker Recipes
  by Donna-Marie Pye
- Canada's Best Slow Cooker Recipes
  by Donna-Marie Pye
- The Best Family Slow Cooker Recipes
  by Donna-Marie Pye
- 125 Best Indoor Grill Recipes
  by Ilana Simon
- The Best Convection Oven Cookbook
  by Linda Stephen
- 125 Best Toaster Oven Recipes
  by Linda Stephen
- 250 Best American Bread Machine Baking Recipes
  by Donna Washburn and Heather Butt
- 250 Best Canadian Bread Machine Baking Recipes
  by Donna Washburn and Heather Butt

- 250 Best Cobblers, Custards, Cupcakes, Bread Puddings & more
  Esther Brody

Baking

- 250 Best Cakes & Pies
  by Esther Brody
- 250 Best Cobblers, Custards, Cupcakes, Bread Puddings & More
  by Esther Brody
- 500 Best Cookies, Bars & Squares
  by Esther Brody
- 500 Best Muffin Recipes
  by Esther Brody
- 125 Best Cheesecake Recipes
  by George Geary
- 125 Best Chocolate Recipes
  by Julie Hasson
- 125 Best Chocolate Chip Recipes
  by Julie Hasson
- Cake Mix Magic
  by Jill Snider
- Cake Mix Magic 2
  by Jill Snider

Healthy Cooking

- 125 Best Vegetarian Recipes
  by Byron Ayanoglu with contributions from Alexis Kemezys
- The Juicing Bible
  by Pat Crocker and Susan Eagles
- The Smoothies Bible
  by Pat Crocker
- Better Baby Food
  by Daina Kalnins, RD, CNSD and Joanne Saab, RD
- Better Food for Kids
  by Daina Kalnins, RD, CNSD and Joanne Saab, RD

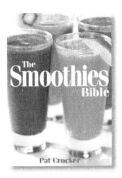

- 500 Best Healthy Recipes
  Edited by Lynn Roblin, RD
- 125 Best Gluten-Free Recipes
  by Donna Washburn and Heather Butt
- America's Everyday Diabetes Cookbook
  Edited by Katherine E. Younker, MBA, RD
- Canada's Everyday Diabetes Choice Recipes
  Edited by Katherine E. Younker, MBA, RD
- The Diabetes Choice Cookbook for Canadians
  Edited by Katherine E. Younker, MBA, RD
- The Best Diabetes Cookbook (U.S.)
  Edited by Katherine E. Younker, MBA, RD

Recent Bestsellers

- 300 Best Comfort Food Recipes
  by Johanna Burkhard
- The Convenience Cook
  by Judith Finlayson
- The Spice and Herb Bible
  by Ian Hemphill
- 125 Best Ice Cream Recipes
  by Marilyn Linton and Tanya Linton
- 125 Best Casseroles & One-Pot Meals
  by Rose Murray
- The Cook's Essential Kitchen Dictionary
  by Jacques Rolland

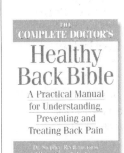

- 125 Best Ground Meat Recipes
  by Ilana Simon
- Easy Indian Cooking
  by Suneeta Vaswani
- Simply Thai Cooking
  by Wandee Young and Byron Ayanoglu

Health

- The Complete Natural Medicine Guide to the 50 Most Common Medicinal Herbs
  by Dr. Heather Boon, B.Sc.Phm., Ph.D. and Michael Smith, B.Pharm, M.R.Pharm.S., ND
- The Complete Kid's Allergy and Asthma Guide
  Edited by Dr. Milton Gold
- The Complete Natural Medicine Guide to Breast Cancer
  by Sat Dharam Kaur, ND
- The Complete Doctor's Stress Solution
  by Penny Kendall-Reed, MSc, ND and Dr. Stephen Reed, MD, FRCSC
- The Complete Doctor's Healthy Back Bible
  by Dr. Stephen Reed, MD and Penny Kendall-Reed, MSc, ND with Dr. Michael Ford, MD, FRCSC and Dr. Charles Gregory, MD, ChB, FRCP(C)
- Everyday Risks in Pregnancy & Breastfeeding
  by Dr. Gideon Koren, MD, FRCP(C), ND

Also Available
from Robert Rose

250 BEST
Cakes &
Pies

Esther Brody